Rejoice

The Journey to Joy and Peace

The greatness we carry motivates us to live through tragedy and trauma courageously. From this place of courage emerges a resilient spirit led onward to experience

An abundant life of Joy and Peace!

Janice Selene Thornton-Hubbard

Rejoice
The Journey to Joy and Peace
All Rights Reserved.
Copyright © 2024 Janice Selene Thornton-Hubbard
v3.0

The opinions expressed in this manuscript are solely the opinions of the author and do not represent the opinions or thoughts of the publisher. The author has represented and warranted full ownership and/or legal right to publish all the materials in this book.

This book may not be reproduced, transmitted, or stored in whole or in part by any means, including graphic, electronic, or mechanical without the express written consent of the publisher except in the case of brief quotations embodied in critical articles and reviews.

Brainstorm Workz

Use Your QR App
To Learn More Today

Paperback ISBN: 979-8-218-97871-6
Hardback ISBN: 979-8-218-97872-3

Cover Photo © 2024 www.gettyimages.com. All rights reserved - used with permission.

PRINTED IN THE UNITED STATES OF AMERICA

Today is the first day of the best days of your life!

*This book is dedicated
to all my special friends and family and
to those who live courageous and resilient lives
despite the trauma of the loss
of one or more children.*

*In loving memory
of three inspiring, powerful women
whose lives reflected
Greatness, Courage, and Resilience:
Pastor Carrie James, Ms. Jenetta Walker,
and Sharon Renee Thornton Workman.*

Everyone needs inspiration in their lives.
I release my inspiration, Joy, and Peace
that surrounds me every day of my life!
Through natural and supernatural events
Rejoice guided me into an experience
to showcase a book
that continues to stabilize me throughout my journey.

Rejoice is informative, insightful, and
motivational
wisdom, guiding every reader
toward joy and peace!

I dare you to Rejoice and
live an abundant life!
Live, Laugh, and be well!
It is your time, a time you have to Rejoice!

Table of Contents

Chapter 1: The Abundant Life Connection

Chapter 2: Focus, The Posture of Joy

Chapter 3: Everything Starts With You

Chapter 4: Supernatural Encounters

Chapter 5: The Love Factor

Chapter 6: A Prophetic Insight of Seasons

Chapter 7: Dance Partners

Chapter 8: Weight Watchers

Chapter 9: Spark Joy

Chapter 1

The Abundant Life Connection

Rejoice! Clap your hands! Sing the New Song! Lift your hands and Bless His holy name! Dance and joy in the God of your salvation. For this is the day that the Lord has made. Let us rejoice and be glad in it! Lift your voice with a shout of praise! Hallelujah! Open up your mouth and Bless His Holy name! Magnify the Lord with me, for He is good, and His Mercy endures forever! Hallelujah! The gospel singer/songwriter Israel Houghton sang, "Rejoice in the Lord, always and again I say, again I say, Rejoice." "Come bless the Lord. Draw near to worship Christ, the Lord, and bless His name, His Holy name declaring He is good!" An incarcerated man was the inspiration behind this song. He wrote a letter to a specific group, saying: Rejoice in the Lord always, and again, I say Rejoice. Why would an incarcerated man unjustly imprisoned say Rejoice? This man was formerly destroying and killing people who had the truth.

Rejoice

Until the day he had a supernatural encounter with God Almighty that transformed his thinking, behavior, and belief system. The purpose of his life was so significant to humanity that he would be used to write a portion of the Bible. The responsibility he was given and accepted came with a price. He endured extreme hardship, persecution, and unjust circumstances like his incarceration. What did he know? What did he understand? He knew that his unfair circumstances were temporary. Paul understood and believed that to be absent from his body meant he would be present with God. He was not afraid to die and was content with dying because he knew that his destination would be the presence of God. His faith in God was solid. He was a man pursued by the Most High God who surrendered his life to God's purpose. Paul developed an intimate relationship with God, gaining spiritual revelation and insight. During his incarceration, he not only gave instructions to Rejoice but also told the people to shift their focus. He told them to think about things that are lovely, just, true, honest, pure, and of an excellent report. Paul is showing us the abundant life connection to overcoming circumstances and tribulation. What connects us to abundance is seeing beyond what is apparent and speaking what should be our focus! Paul had learned how to live a life of joy regardless of his circumstances, and so can you and me. We are privileged today because we can access the God of all flesh. The Great I Am has given us the right to access His unspeakable joy from the presence of His Holy Spirit.

Today is the day you can enter an experience with pleasure and have a new life. This Great God gives us a reason to Rejoice. He awakens us daily to a new day full of His grace, goodness, and mercy. We can embrace the purpose in each day we are given. We can do this when our hearts are open to the truth. The truth is we are here living and breathing with the breath of life given to us by God, the Master Creator. He is the one who created the day that belongs to Him.

This intentional God gives us daily opportunities for self-discovery, intimacy with Him, and living our purpose. We should pursue His presence in a celebratory posture because He extends His incredible kindness to us. God sees you and me in suffering and cares about every human being. It is encouraging to know that He cares about all our life distresses, those anxieties, sorrows, and the pain we experience. We don't have to remain stuck in the distress of life. Instead, we can frame our day with what is good and beautiful because everything has beauty. Set your sight on His love for you, and never forget He surrounds you with His love! When you call Him, He will answer and be with you when you are in trouble! Acknowledge God daily and recognize His sovereign power is present in your life. Rejoice in the life of Jesus Christ, the Son of the living God, the gateway to life, freedom, and satisfaction. He came into this world to save all humanity and give us everything we need. He came to provide us with an abundant life that is full and good.

Rejoice

I am grateful for all He has done for me, and I am living a posture of abundance, a life filled with joy and peace. I align my life with the book that has significantly influenced how I navigate my course. The words of this book are alive and tangible. Its transforming power inspires positive results. This book holds insights into addressing problems and instructs us on how to live our lives. All the issues of our day are contained within the pages of this book, beginning from the very first book called Genesis. It is profound to me that this book operates like a map to guide our direction and yet is an eternal power impacting our spiritual and natural destiny. In the pages of Rejoice, you will see my personal experiences and the connection to my intimate relationship with God. He is a personable God who connects one thing to another. Connection is powerful! Connection is a relational dynamic. This great God is a relationship expert who intentionally knows how to join us in successful relationships. When we encounter people we can gain a deep connection with, our experience becomes an abundant life. When strong people and those with a deep sense of purpose enter our lives, we experience a productive life. Healthy relationships will help us to live again. I am blessed to have new, trustworthy relationships. My new relationships are an act of divine providence and an answer to prayer. These relationships are helping me to grow beyond my borders. As I embrace each person the Lord sends, I know our exchange produces what I need in my life and theirs.

The purpose of relationships is to help us grow in every aspect of who we are. Through my choice to accept Jesus Christ into my life, I have gained a relationship that connects me with everything I need. The kind of life I experience with Jesus is full and good.

This relationship has become my foundation and gives me the capacity to have the wisdom to navigate my other relationships. This life I call abundant is a life of joy.

This joy in me is from God and is why I am strong. Life circumstances, challenges, and adversity have been plenteous, yet none could take me out. What about you?

How do you navigate life's many challenges? How do we connect with an abundant life amidst the many trials?

What about the troubles we see others going through, which shakes us to the core? There are many courageous people living today who grieve the loss of a child. It is difficult to speak to this kind of trauma, and I pray I never have to. But for those who have, I empathetically say that each day, you get up, breathe, cry, and do whatever you must to live well. I don't know that you can ever get over the loss of a child. God, who says children are a gift from him, cares. He is with you and will demonstrate His love for you if you let Him. He is always close to the broken-hearted.

Rejoice

Through the traumatic events of your life, God's love will be an anchor to your soul. He is with you now, caring for you in all your distress and suffering. His faithful love towards you will continue to hold you close. His love is surrounding your heart to strengthen you. We need joy when we suffer through hard times because His joy is strength! The source of this joy is love. This joy manifests from agape love, love that loves without a condition. There have been times when trouble was all around me, and that joy would bubble up within me, manifesting in laughter. This laughter comes from the presence of the Holy Spirit.

I MARVEL when I ponder my connection with God's spirit, the Holy Spirit. Although I cannot see Him, His presence is always near, and He responds to me when I call on Him, asking for help. My connection with the Holy Spirit has deepened as I have spent time in the book's pages that have inspired me to live. This book has brought me deep inner healing and continues to do so. One of the best connections I have experienced is within this book, and connection is a gift God gives us daily. We have this opportunity to connect deeply with Him and others. In 2023, I experienced a multitude of deep connections.

While at the park one day, I met a 3-year-old girl who extended her arms to embrace me with a hug. This baby reached to hug me three more times and then gave me a high-five.

I just happened to see this 3-year-old baby again in the same place. Amazingly, it was the same child. She hugged me more times this time and said it was nice to meet me. I met an older woman who offered me kind words. She told me to let my light keep shining. In another encounter, an 11-year-old girl told me I was beautiful. Were these connections random? Of course not. These encounters were intentional and remarkably profound and orchestrated by God. I was experiencing His kisses through human beings. We all need these moments when someone comes along and touches us with love. I have had many other experiences like these, but more connections with needy people. Sometimes, I have wondered why these connections are essential; however, I do not discount any of them. God is intentionally and strategically orchestrating divine moments for each of us. If we choose to be aware of all that surrounds us, that awareness inspires us to see how one thing connects to another. Have you ever considered how one part of our physical body connects with another to ensure proper function?

It amazes me that God created the parts of our human body to communicate with other parts for its functionality. Can you see His intentionality? Can you see how important connection is to Him?

Everyone wants connection, and we know this because we all carry an inward desire to belong to something or someone.

Rejoice

Every human wants to be loved, seen, heard, and valued. If you have met people who bring out the best in you, know that God is involved in your meeting these people. He knows what we all need. Value those who enter your life with whom you find a deep connection because your exchange with them will bring meaning to your life. Value these relationships because some of them may only be for a season. Every deep connection you make has a significant purpose. These relationships can bring joy and hope, replacing the sorrow and heartache from despair and grief. In October last year, I met another stranger while writing this book, and the words she spoke to me touched me deeply. She said kind words to me while sharing a need. I asked her if she and I could pray together in agreement for God to meet her needs. We prayed together, and I believe God will do what she asked. Ms. Doris is an elderly widow, and because of the recent loss of her husband, she wants to live closer to the beautiful park where we met. Ms. Doris told me it is important to speak to everyone in her encounters because her voice may be the only voice that person hears. This beautiful soul also said to me despite the loss of her husband, she chooses to live in joy. I was grateful she was a part of my inspiration that day, along with the sunshine and river I sat admiring. We will have all kinds of challenging moments and circumstances as we live. However, just like this elderly widow, we have the power to choose. I love that she decides to live in the presence of joy. She can only do this because of her connection with God.

What about you? Are you experiencing heartbreak? Are you challenged by circumstances you have no control over? Is your heart filled with sorrow and despair? The challenges you face right now can defeat you if you choose to let them. Why should you sorrow in what you cannot control? You can choose joy over sorrow, faith over fear, peace over chaos, and hope over despair. Joy is a choice, just as sorrow is. Our sufferings can wipe us out or bring us into a victorious, thriving place. Our choices, whether positive or negative, determine our outcomes. Most often, when something terrible happens, we talk about it. If we tell more than one person, we are rehearsing it. While it is necessary sometimes to express our troubles, we must not allow these troubles to become the focus of our communication. May we take harmful, toxic, unhealthy thoughts and knock them out of our minds. Our victory journey begins when we shift our focus and center it on what is good in a bad situation. Let me give you a great example of this. Last year, I visited my extraordinary friends who have been married for 30 years. In 2020, their oldest son, Andrew, passed away. It was such a disheartening loss for them and for all who knew their son.

However, my friends decided to change the narrative of their tragic experience. Since Andrew's passing, they have built a restaurant and named it AJ's Comfort Food, LLC. The restaurant sits next to their beautiful home in Lincoln, Delaware.

Andrew's father always wanted to own a restaurant, and his parents decided this would be the way to keep their son's memory alive.

As I encountered them, I was uplifted and inspired by their decision to live beyond such a loss. They are both full of joy, and their community will be significantly encouraged as they encounter the comfort foods the couple will provide. I was encouraged to see my special friends decide to live intentionally in purpose, not tragedy. They had made a concerted decision together to live above the pain they experienced. It is evident in their actions that they are a healthy-minded couple who refuse to bow to grief and entertain negative thinking. What we think affects everything about us and how well we live. Our minds, the part of us that we often neglect, is connected to our thoughts. If we want to live well, we must practice thinking healthy thoughts. Negativity is debilitating, but joy is restorative. Negativity weakens our ability to be strong, but joy operates in us as strength. We must apply spiritual and natural means to improve our thoughts. The power of the Bible's words changes how we think if we speak them repetitively. Meditating on God's word is a way of encouraging ourselves effectively and addressing negative thinking.

We all have moments of weakness, sorrow, and unpleasant thoughts of experiences that have shaken us at the core of our being.

However, we must choose joy to increase our capacity to live a vibrant, healthy life like the elderly widow I spoke about and my friends who experienced the loss of their son. We must create our own space to live our best life. Identify where your thoughts gravitate and shift them toward looking at the good in something terrible. If you quickly see the negative in the circumstances and never look for anything good, you practice unhealthy thinking. Sometimes, we need to talk about things that are hard to release. Sometimes, writing your thoughts down or speaking about them can be helpful. Both of these steps are ways of removing what is troubling you. Either way, you can decide to get rid of it. If you write it down, you can throw it away. If you talk it out, you can let it go. Letting it go means it is no longer having space in your thoughts. You don't have to talk about it anymore. Letting go is really about releasing negativity.

In November last year, I saw an older man I met in 2021 while walking in the park. I walked daily in the park in 2021 to address my physical and emotional health. When I met this gentleman, he had shared about the loss of his son to suicide. He was troubled and sorrowful. But when I saw him this time, he looked well and whole. I spoke with him, and he remembered me. He made some profound comments that I will not forget. He said, "All we need to do is love one another because we are in this world together." He also said, "Mental illness is real, but my son did not know how to release the negativity."

Rejoice

Then he said," We must release the negativity." I heard him clearly, and I ask you to do the same. Now, let your focus be on what is good and positive. Your focus is vital to your health and strength because there is a connection between your mind and focus. Remember to reflect on the good in your circumstance, not the circumstance itself. Reflecting on the positive in a bad situation is practicing gratitude. I have given testimony in the past several years of hard things I have survived, and when I share, I seek to focus on communicating the good that came out of the circumstance.

I generally do this well if it is written on paper because I have time to think about how I want to articulate it. Recently, I encountered a lovely stranger in the parking lot of a grocery store I was preparing to enter.

I initially began encouraging her as I sensed she needed support. This lady was just as sensitive and attempted to redirect my conversation with her to a more favorable position. I thought she needed to hear my multitude of testimonies. Somehow, I got in the way of what I should have said as my mind shifted quickly to share. My testimonies were not communicated as victories because my mind had moved to the details of the traumatic events. At one point, the lady said the word trauma. At the same time, saying the word trauma, she acknowledged to me that I was still alive, standing in the sun, sharing with her.

She quickly discerned the negative focus I had unknowingly positioned myself into and respectfully excused herself. I felt so bad, but I was glad she did what she did. I did not realize that my thoughts had shifted, becoming centered on all the bad. Although I am usually more focused when verbally communicating with others, I missed it with this lady. I walked away, telling myself to remember to be sensitive to the leading of God because He knows what we all need. I dislike it when people are insensitive, yet I practiced what I disliked during this encounter. I didn't even realize that my mind and thoughts were not solid at the present moment until I had the conversation with the lady. Our minds can control how we live, and our thoughts can shape the life we experience. Keeping negative details of circumstances in our focus is unfruitful. The consequences of carrying adverse circumstances can be dire. We have the power to shift our thoughts to something positive. It may seem like you have to do this continually. It is okay; just change from negative to positive. Negative thoughts tend to come to me in the morning as I awaken, and I immediately redirect my thoughts to being grateful that I awakened. I think about things that I have been fortunate to have survived. Reflecting on the things I have lived through, I redirect my focus to how I got through them, not what happened. In the mornings, when I awaken, I begin to sing because music can move my thoughts and mind in a positive direction. I also get out of bed and start declaring positive affirmations over myself. Music is powerful and vital to our lives.

Rejoice

You can feel uplifted when choosing songs with the right words. I also dance till freedom in my thoughts comes and sing till joy releases within my heart. I get outdoors and stroll by a nearby river. I intentionally get into the moment, soaking up the sun's rays as I watch nature respond to its environment.

At night, I play a 12-hour meditation with scriptures from the bible and a 12-hour meditation with rain sounds. I play the 12-hour meditation low enough to hear it and not keep me awake. The meditation I use with Bible scriptures helps me fall asleep quickly and is helpful in my staying physically and emotionally whole. These are some of the tools I have used, which have worked tremendously for me. Again, I want you to realize that your mind and thoughts connect with your body. Connection: this is the vehicle that drives us into abundant living when we connect to what brings us abundance.

> *Philippians 4:4* (AMP) *Rejoice in the Lord always [delight, take pleasure in Him]; again, I will say, rejoice!*
>
> *Psalms 118:24* (CSB) *This is the day the Lord has made; let's rejoice and be glad in it.*
>
> *2 Corinthians 5:8* (NKJV) *We are confident, yes, well pleased rather to be absent from the body and to be present with the Lord.*

Psalm 127:3 (TLB) Children are a gift from God; they are his reward.

Psalms 34:18 (NLT) The Lord is close to the brokenhearted; he rescues those whose spirits are crushed.

Psalms 31:7 (AMP) I will rejoice and be glad in Your steadfast love, Because You have seen my affliction; You have taken note of my life's distresses.

1 Thessalonians 5:16-18,22 (CSB) Rejoice always, pray constantly, give thanks in everything; for this is God's will for you in Christ Jesus. Stay away from every kind of evil.

John 10:9-10 B (ERV) A thief comes to steal, kill, and destroy. But I came to give life—life that is full and good.

Chapter 2

Focus, The Posture of Joy

I learned many years ago how to take the posture of joy. Love is my mantra, and joy and peace flow from my life to others. As I write this book about His wonders, I am full of His joy! Yes, I am jumping for joy, laughing and dancing, thanking and praising Him from my heart. "Jesus, you're the center of my joy. All that's good and perfect comes from you. You're the heart of my contentment and hope for all I do. Jesus, you're the center of my Joy. When I heard the voice of the Lord in 1990, he said, "The call of my life was singing." The first song I sang solo in the needy environment I worked in was Jesus, You're the Center of My Joy by Richard Smallwood. My employer permitted me to sing that song with a local singing group who had come to minister. From that moment of saying yes to God, I sang throughout my career at work for over 24 1/2 years. Every time I opened my mouth to sing, I deposited the presence of joy into that environment. I became a reservoir of God's presence.

Rejoice

My posture of singing to God had become my posture of joy. Although my life journey patterns tragedy and triumph, worship was and continues to be my weapon. The joy of the Lord in me is how I got over the tragedies to the place of victory. God clothed me with His joy, turning my mourning into dancing. He gave me songs of victory; new songs flooded my heart. I cannot talk with you about joy without talking about tragedy and trauma because they are a part of the process of this life. Jesus Christ made a profound statement that I think about often. Jesus said, "In this world, you will have tribulation, but be of good cheer, for I have overcome the world." There are several things I hear from His profound words. He references this world, which indicates that there is another world. Secondly, Jesus speaks of tribulation in this world. Tribulation is both tragedy and trauma. It is suffering, sorrow, and pain. Jesus experienced all this at the hands of men on the way to the place where He was crucified. Scriptures tell us that Jesus was physically beaten beyond recognition and spit upon. The evil-spirited people placed a crown of thorns on His head. He endured the most painful death known to man while the people surrounding the cross mocked and insulted Him. Imagine someone placing you on a cross, driving nails forcefully into your hands and feet to keep your body mounted. Jesus was pierced in His side with a sword and hung on a tree to die. Yet through all He experienced, He tells us to be of good cheer because He overcame it all. Jesus is saying that through His death and resurrection, He has deprived tribulation of its power to harm us and conquered it for us.

Like Jesus, we can all identify with tragedy, trauma, sorrow, and pain. Yet we are victorious in every tribulation, even death, because Jesus sacrificed His life for ours.

Looking into history-makers' lives, we see their tragedy and trauma. Leaders like Martin Luther King, Harriet Tubman, Nelson Mandela, United States President Abraham Lincoln, and our current President, Joseph Biden, also experienced triumph and victory. The common thread between them was courage, the courage to see beyond their tribulation! Courage pushed them towards victory and triumph.

We can also take a tragic moment and bring beauty out of our pain. One of the greatest influencers of our time, Oprah Winfrey, said, "Turn your wounds into wisdom." She shared these powerful words alongside her subject matter of getting her opportunity to act. Oprah's first acting role was in "The Color Purple." The backdrop of the film was sexual abuse in a family. Oprah never mentions the sexual abuse when she speaks about turning your wounds into wisdom. However, she told her audience she would have done anything to get a role in this movie. Oprah knew the storyline of "The Color Purple" patterned her personal life, yet she was courageous enough to break through the trauma that wounded her early in life. Her determination to overcome brought her to the position of triumph and victory! Her desire to become an actress fueled her towards freedom.

Oprah's drive to help others towards freedom was motivated by the freedom she experienced. What do you possess that can break you through the limitations, struggles, and difficulties trauma has caused you? What do you carry that can contribute to other's traumatic experiences?

Jesus said to be courageous, be confident, and be undaunted. He told us not to be afraid, intimidated, and discouraged when facing difficulty, danger, and disappointment. After Jesus tells us this in John 16:33, He also says to be filled with joy. Think about what Jesus has said. Be filled with joy. How do we become full of joy in the presence of trauma? You must believe God works to bring good out of everything, including evil. He will do this for those who love Him and those He has called for His purpose. To live full of joy, you must have the Holy Spirit, the producer of joy and peace. The only way you can experience His joy and peace is to give Him your sorrow, pain, and depression. You must hand it over to Him, and He will release joy and peace upon you. He will give you Beauty for your Ashes and pour the oil of His joy upon your heart! He will clothe you with praise, but you must lift your voice and sing! The igniter of joy is singing. As an act of surrender, if you lift your hands, open your mouth, and sing, joy will manifest. The Holy Spirit is the Spirit of truth who will guide you into all truth. He is the helper who teaches us all things and brings to our memory what Jesus has told us.

If you let Him, He will lead, comfort, and guide you daily, helping you walk out your spiritual journey in power. The Bible also reveals the Holy Spirit as the Spirit of love and power. The way to access joy and peace is through love. When God's love operates from your heart, joy and peace become tangibly present, flowing from you to others. Live in and demonstrate Godly love (unconditional love) to receive joy for yourself and release joy to others.

God has not given us the spirit of fear, nor would He because fear is a demonic spirit. We need the presence of the Holy Spirit because He will help us harness and control our minds. With the Holy Spirit, we can live strong in our human spirit and control the part of us that does not want to do what is right: our flesh. God wants us to receive gifts from Him. The Holy Spirit is a gift from God, and He comes to live in our hearts when we accept the gift of salvation, God's saving power! However, we must first be willing to accept the gift of salvation. There are two steps to receive this gift. First, we must say from our mouths that Jesus is the Lord and acknowledge He is the Son of the Living God. Second, we must believe in and with our hearts that God raised Jesus from the dead. To experience God's rescuing power, simply ask God to save you and forgive you of your sinful ways. There is an immediate rescue from yourself and the sin nature you were born in.

Confessing your need for God with your mouth and believing He had the power to resurrect Jesus from death releases His salvation, His saving power to you! Now, that is the kind of news I want to think about and talk about. Knowing what Jesus did for us and how God wants to save us with His power should be our focus! You can choose to think about things that are the best, not the worst; the beautiful, not the ugly, things to praise, not things to curse. Maintaining a joyful posture requires focus to think and speak the right thing. If you begin your day with joy and distractions show up, your happiness will wane. You have to stop all of the distractions in your daily routine. Distractions are a strategy linked to people, your to-do list, and sometimes unexpected events. Our relationships and the people connected to us can be a source of sorrow, depleting our joy. The apostle Paul, who wrote a large portion of the New Testament of the Bible we read today, experienced relationship issues written in scripture. However, Paul had a focus that kept him on track. I know people you trusted the most let you down. I understand people have done things to you and said things that caused you to see yourself as unworthy and without value. I am not minimizing what you have experienced in your life. But if Paul, who was human like us, could look beyond the apparent and focus on the good, we can, too. Despite your painful experiences, begin to set boundaries around your life. Then you will see what you need to do. Your next steps will become clear.

The stress you may be experiencing will diminish. Boundaries are necessary because the people in your life may need to do the same for themselves. Remember, boundaries are tools for self-development and healthy relationships. You will have the time to appreciate the gift of time when others do not overload you. Although you encounter people who do not show you value, do not let them push on you what they think of themselves. Release yourself from other people's expectations. Keep the right focus because your focus connects to what you believe. Did you know your belief system, like your thoughts, focus, and decisions, determines your life course? Is your belief system empowering, or is it limiting? My empowering belief system is to honor God, love people, and walk out the greatness I carry to impact the world.

How do we achieve the most incredible sense of identity, purpose, and meaning in life? It begins with love for God, love for yourself, and love for people. My passion for people has grown as I grow in my love for God. Love embraces others.

I choose to embrace every person because I want that embrace reciprocated. We all fail in our relationships sometimes because of unrealistic expectations. However, we must accept people where they are even when they display poor behavior. Otherwise, how will they know the incredible love God has for them?

They will only know His love through those who will accept and embrace them where they are. God has a love for us that's accepting and embracing! He loves us where we are, and we are changed when we receive His love. Although I readily embrace others, I listen carefully to determine whether the person is a friend or foe. I lean on the Holy Spirit, and if I get uneasy, I pray and ask the Holy Spirit to show me the person's heart. We can discover who someone is by what they talk about and what they do. If a person means to harm me, I simply back up from them. I hope you understand that all these things stop the flow of joy. The way we think about things, unrealistic expectations, an unhealthy belief system, repeated abuse, unresolved trauma, manipulative, controlling, and negative people are all robbers of joy. While we will not get away from encountering people detrimental to us, we should carefully consider who will be in our inner circle. Master handling people with kindness. Being unkind when someone is unkind to me is not necessary. I can stand against the negativity and cruelty of people with compassion, a warm embrace, and positivity in my thoughts. I can show them something that they do not know; I can show them love.

Offering a person kindness is a way of showing them love; however, hanging out with them is not an option. The ability to maintain your joy happens when you move away from negative people who are professionals who create negative situations.

I am inspired not to let evil circumstances define me. Wicked people can traumatize you, so use wisdom and be intentional about who you bring close to you. Many of us have had traumatic experiences like Oprah Winfrey. I know it was not easy for her. It is not easy for anyone who has lived with any form of abuse. It takes time for us to heal. It takes some people years, partly because it is difficult to let go of it. For others, it can take years to experience freedom because of repeated abuse. Despite it all, the most important thing is that we do not allow the trauma to define us. Unresolved trauma and abuse can destroy us, leading us to an early death, or it can make us a force to contend with. You should push past what is dark in your life. I refuse to let darkness win. I am determined to see the light on the other side. What about you? Each morning, we awaken to light coming in from the dark. The light pushes through the darkness to light our path for that day. Whether the day is negative or positive, I am intentional about what I say. For example, I do not walk around telling everyone I am sick. It is okay to say you are not feeling well; just don't rehearse it because you don't want to give it life.

Have you ever noticed that when you say you are sick, you tend to say it multiple times, and before you know it, you become sicker? I often tell myself that I am healthy and whole and tell the illness to go away. When my mom was alive and became ill, she also became disabled. However, she never spoke about it from her mouth.

Many times, she demonstrated courage and determination against the terminal disease that was killing her. She had a strong spirit and did not fold easily. I may experience illness, but I do not have to accept it and declare it, and neither should you. As 2022 exited and 2023 came in, I decided I would not watch unhealthy television programs. I have also limited my television viewing time to shows and movies that present positive information. I want nothing being sown into me to stifle the joy and peace in my heart. I want my mind and thoughts to be free of negative imagery. Repeatedly watching violence can also cause us to become desensitized. We see it every day when we go into public places. People are rude, unkind, and violent. We see it on our highways, where people use their cars as weapons through road rage, recklessness, and lawlessness.

Besides, the battle we are all engaged in daily is the battle for our minds. Yes, there is a sinister strategy at work with one goal, and that is to infiltrate our minds to give access to demonic forces and their influence. I am giving you two strategies to receive and operate by. I have already shared how to continually access joy and peace, which is your spiritual strategy. What I am sharing now is your natural strategy. Be aggressive about protecting your eyes and ears. If our thoughts are negative, those thoughts are attached to a circumstance or something we have seen or heard.

I am training myself to deal with whatever happened that was negative so I don't hold onto it in my mind and thoughts. Storms, adversity, and circumstances shift our focus and influence us to speak about them instead of what is good. It cannot become greater and accelerate in power if you don't give it attention. In 2022, I decided not to accept phone calls after 8 pm because I noticed that, as people, we all tend to be insensitive. At this time, I start to prepare myself for rest and sleep. Nor do I accept any phone calls or text messages containing negative information in the evening hours. If I am going to talk about something impactful, I talk about it during the early part of the day. I do not want anything interfering with my internal peace or my ability to sleep at night. I have become intentional about my communication with others. If I know someone leans towards talking about negative things, I generally avoid conversing with them. I am not talking about someone who may be having a bad day. We all have bad days. When we have a bad day, we must remember to shake it off, but we don't have to do this alone. Sometimes, you can connect to someone to help you escape that negative situation, trying to become a part of your mind. Are you battling with negativity? If you apply the spiritual and natural strategies I share, you will live free. You do not have to remain negative, but you must choose not to be your worst enemy. Do what I have done.

Make the right choice and Rejoice! You should want to feel good in your mind, thoughts, and body. I love my new life!

Understand you are battling negativity because you allow it to speak to you. Just get up and shift to what is positive because it is good for your spirit, soul, and body. The battle within our minds and thoughts is working to sabotage every area of our lives. The evil strategy destroys our health, relationships, and even our finances. An unhealthy mind means an unhealthy physical body.

If you are the person who says, "I am not the one! I am putting a stop to this madness right now!" Let me tell you, when you operate like this, you will overthrow the limited thinking and negative thoughts. However, to maintain your freedom, you must be relentless in your efforts because evil forces are also relentless. I encourage you to invest in a Bible titled "Battlefield of the Mind" by Joyce Meyers!" It is one of my best Bibles, which I use because it is relevant to our daily lives. Joyce Meyers Bible is easy to follow and simply explains the scriptures addressing our life experiences. The word of God will transform you, and you will stop being a garbage truck, a container of negative words. The word of God will shift you on the inside to being so sensitive that you will not treat people like they are trash cans you can dump garbage into. You will leave people better than you found them. Remember, what you put out comes back to you. If you don't speak negatively to others, you will not have negative words returned to you. The spiritual law of sowing and reaping is fundamental. Please take heed and listen carefully to what I am saying.

Focus, The Posture of Joy

You cannot change a spiritual law, so only put out what you want to return to you. Pay attention to yourself and what you are thinking and speaking. Some people are constant talkers and may have a deep, unfulfilled need. You may encounter someone like this, and you can gently guide them towards a positive conversation. Reposition your communication to keep the flame of joy lit in you. Everything you speak is attached to your focus. Your focus is just as important as your thoughts. I used to wonder why the news is repetitive in communication, but now I know that repeated information is strategic. Negative news and negative information on repeat are strategies. Think about it. You are a faithful news watcher, repeatedly seeing and hearing the same negative information. Do you think you can maintain a positive focus when subjecting yourself to these words? Repeated bad news creates depression, fear, and sadness. Do you watch the news late at night before bed? Get rid of this self-sabotaging habit that results in poor sleep. You will not remain physically healthy if you don't get quality sleep. A lack of sleep also impacts you mentally and emotionally. Keep news watching to a minimum; just do not watch it every day and not at night before bed. I refrain from watching the news because I often repeat what I heard or saw from the information presented. Guess what? I was broadcasting the negative report I heard and observed. It had become a seed sown in me. You will know it is a seed in you because it will be what you talk about.

Rejoice

Because I have become relentless against negativity occupying space in my heart, I now have an experience of freedom that promotes greater productivity. My heart is changing, and my inner life is experiencing restoration. I see it, I sense it, and I feel it every day. You can, too.

Remember that your words and those of others impact your heart, and your thoughts affect your life. Stay connected to God's presence! Keep your focus and heart on Him, and keep your heart clean and free of negativity, including negative people and unhealthy self-talk. Speak life, speak positive words, and you will bring it into reality. Do not speak what you do not wish to become a reality because you will have what you say. Keep your joy ignited through worship. Rejoice in Him! Delight in His presence and stay in praise and dance! Worship God because it indeed opens the doors to all God's goodness! As you experience His goodness towards you, His unspeakable joy in you will overflow abundantly!

> *Psalms 9:1-2* (MSG) *I'm thanking you, God, from a full heart. I'm writing the book on your wonders. I'm whistling, laughing, and jumping for joy; I'm singing your song, High God.*
>
> *Psalms 30:11* (AMP) *You have turned my mourning into dancing for me; You have taken off my sackcloth and clothed me with joy.*

John 16:33 (NKJV) "These things I have spoken to you, that in Me you may have peace. In the world you will have tribulation; but be of good cheer, I have overcome the world."

Read Mark 15:16-39 (ERV) This is an account of Jesus's crucifixion and death.

John 16:33 (AMP) "I have told you these things, so that in Me you may have [perfect] peace. In the world you have tribulation and distress and suffering, but be courageous [be confident, be undaunted, be filled with joy]; I have overcome the world." [My conquest is accomplished, My victory abiding.]

Romans 8:28 (GNT) We know that in all things God works for good with those who love him, those whom he has called according to his purpose.

Isaiah 61:3 (NKJV) "To comfort all who mourn, To console those who mourn in Zion, To give them beauty for ashes, The oil of joy for mourning, The garment of praise for the spirit of heaviness; That they may be called trees of righteousness, The planting of the Lord, that He may be glorified."

Rejoice

John 16:13 (NLT) When the Spirit of truth comes, he will guide you into all truth. He will not speak on his own but will tell you what he has heard. He will tell you about the future.

John 14:26 (NKJV) But the Helper, the Holy Spirit, whom the Father will send in My name, He will teach you all things, and bring to your remembrance all things that I said to you.

2 Timothy 1:7 (CEV) God's Spirit doesn't make cowards out of us. The Spirit gives us power, love, and self-control.

Acts 2:38 (ERV) Peter said to them, "Change your hearts and lives and be baptized, each one of you, in the name of Jesus Christ. Then God will forgive your sins, and you will receive the gift of the Holy Spirit.

Romans 10:9 (AMP) because if you acknowledge and confess with your mouth that Jesus is Lord [recognizing His power, authority, and majesty as God], and believe in your heart that God raised Him from the dead, you will be saved.

Philippians 4:8 (MSG) Summing it all up, friends, I'd say you'll do best by filling your minds and meditating on things true, noble, reputable authentic, compelling, gracious—the best, not the worst; the beautiful, not the ugly; things to praise, not things to curse.

Acts 15:37-39 (ERV) Barnabas wanted to bring John Mark with them too. But on their first trip John Mark did not continue with them in the work. He had left them at Pamphylia. So Paul did not think it was a good idea to take him this time. Paul and Barnabas had a big argument about this. It was so bad that they separated and went different ways. Barnabas sailed to Cyprus and took Mark with him.

Mark 12:30-31 (ERV) Love the Lord your God with all your heart, all your soul, all your mind, and all your strength.'The second most important command is this: 'Love your neighbor the same as you love yourself.' These two commands are the most important."

2 Corinthians 4:6 (GNT) The God who said, "Out of darkness the light shall shine!" is the same God who made his light shine in our hearts, to bring us the knowledge of God's glory shining in the face of Christ.

Rejoice

John 1:5 (ERV) The light shines in the darkness, and the darkness has not defeated it.

Proverbs 18:21 (CEV) Words can bring death or life! Talk too much, and you will eat everything you say.

Hebrews 4:12 (ERV) God's word is alive and working. It is sharper than the sharpest sword and cuts all the way into us. It cuts deep to the place where the soul and the spirit are joined. God's word cuts to the center of our joints and our bones. It judges the thoughts and feelings in our hearts.

Galatians 6:7 (GNBUK) Do not deceive yourselves; no one makes a fool of God. People will reap exactly what they sow.

Psalms 34:9 (MSG) Worship God if you want the best; worship opens doors to all his goodness.

Chapter 3

Everything Starts With You

Who are you, and what do you want in your life? Are you aware of yourself? How do you show up in your relationships? Do you know your value and self-worth? Can you identify your strengths, and can you identify areas of weakness? If it is difficult for you to answer these questions, you may have never created space for yourself, an area where you can see, know, and understand who you are. Or it could be that you take on everyone else's life to meet their needs but never your own. Everything about your life starts with you. You are responsible for who you are, what you want, and how you behave. You are the one who is responsible for seeing your value and worth, and when you do, others will see it, too. I want to encourage you to take time to make space in your life and develop a routine to have your times of reflection. As you reflect, ask yourself these questions to locate how you are living. These questions are vital to you living a healthier life filled with joy. What do you think about the most? Do you think about the good or think more about what is evil? Do you speak positive words or negative words? Do you gossip? When you have a problem with people, are you quick to tell somebody what that person did? Your wrong thinking, talking, and choices will block joy, peace, and success in your life. How you think about things determines your decisions and the things you choose. Having unhealthy relationships will defeat you and deplete you emotionally, psychologically, and mentally, eventually impacting you physically. If you decide wisely, you can prosper emotionally, psychologically, and mentally. Move away from all the people who have been close to you that should not be. You must turn your focus towards you so you can see and hear yourself. Discover yourself so you can shift and turn toward a positively impactful life. The way to live a prosperous journey is to know who you are. The prosperity you need in your life is more than money. Prosperity can be a wallet full of cash. However, how well you live is your wealth. Wealthy and affluent people can attest that their money is not enough to fill the void they recognize inwardly. They can sense the emptiness and identify with it. Their achievements do not bring them lasting joy. Their satisfaction is a temporary experience. A life filled with contentment, peace, and joy is a life of substance. Investing in your mental, psychological, and emotional health gets you on the road to prosperity. We all can have financial wealth if we choose it; however, it shouldn't be our primary motivation.

It is our purpose and our destiny that should be driving us into a life of fulfillment. Your passion lies within your purpose. Everything about you starts with you from the time you were born. Everything that you have experienced as a child moving forward influences how you live today. Should you live from the rearview window instead of the front seat, looking at your painful past?

You are in the driver's seat, driving forward while looking back. How is that working for you? You must know that your destination will bring you to a place you do not want to be. You will undoubtedly crash if you keep your focus in the rearview mirror. Since you are in the driver's seat, you have control, but you have not taken control of the wheel. How about you take control of the steering wheel right now? Now that you have taken control of the wheel, how does it feel to be in control? Yes, I know it feels good, and this is how you must guide your life! Take control of your life, looking ahead and not behind you. Your future is in front of you! Keep your focus forward. You do this by telling yourself daily that you are the only one responsible for your life. Don't keep blaming others for what only you can change. Tell yourself you will not drive your life until it is out of control. Tell yourself you are taking control and moving forward into a bright future full of success, peace, and joy. You have to change the narrative of your life to what you want it to be. It all starts with choosing to obey God's written word.

Rejoice

You must choose to follow God's written word. Your obedience will produce an outcome of peace, and things will go well for you. You will succeed in whatever you choose, and light will shine on the road ahead. These are His words, not mine. I tell myself this is what I want: a life of success, peace, and good opportunities, knowing they will happen as I align with God's standards. You can do the same and have the life you desire and enjoy. Joy and peace will become a part of you, living in your heart. However, you cannot experience joy in your heart when venom comes out of your mouth. Your words are seeds. What you speak is what you will have. You must understand a spiritual law is at work called sowing and reaping. What do you want to reap? If you're going to live long, you must watch the words you speak because speaking negatively about others and yourself will shorten your life. If you are a caring and compassionate person, you must consider how you give yourself in service to others. You cannot be your best when you let everyone around you pull you in every direction. Some people will target you because they will see your generous heart. They prey on you because they think that you are weak. You must know who you are and what your weaknesses are to navigate boundaries. You can still help others, but you are responsible for telling them how you can help them. Never let people tell you how they want your help. You have to decide what is best for you. Pouring your life out in service to people who want what they want when they want it will deplete you.

These people will never come to help you and won't ask you if you need help. My perspective about people is that there are two kinds of people in this world. Some people take, and some people give. People who take are uncaring and tend to be manipulative, controlling, and unloving people. Sometimes, they will let you see their sense of entitlement, and this is where you have to step up. People who display a sense of entitlement are also prideful.

Prideful people will step on you to make themselves look good. They value no one and will try to make you feel wrong if you don't help them.

Although we will encounter prideful, manipulative, uncaring, and unloving people, we do not have to let them control our lives. If you know people like this, and I'm sure you do, then you must back up and regain your steps. It is disheartening to see that we have these behaviors that were not with us at birth. These behaviors develop through our childhood experiences. These learned behaviors become a part of people during childhood due to their dysfunctional environment. If you have these behaviors, get a mentor, a counselor, or someone trustworthy to partner with you to help you address them. They should be someone with a healthy mind and not challenged in your areas of challenge.

Rejoice

A neutral person, such as a professional in mental health, is the best choice because they can provide you with an objective view. Before you can experience a change, prepare yourself to admit your behaviors. This person can help you identify the origin of your behaviors and give you accountability. Accountability is necessary if you want to change yourself because you are the only one who can change you. Some of us tend to feel worried and anxious all the time. From my experiences over the past 13 years, I can assuredly say that if you identify with this type of person, you live in overload. You are living helping everyone because you think you are supposed to help everyone. It is unrealistic, so do not place unrealistic expectations on yourself. You may be the person who wants everyone to like you, so you spend most of your time trying to please others. Get in the driver's seat, take the pleasing people mentality off you, and throw it out the window! Take that Superman and Superwoman cape off and throw it out the window! It is essential to live a life of simplicity, not difficulty. Understanding is as important as wisdom for you to live well. So get this understanding and always remember you will encounter people who will not like you without a cause. People who dislike you without reason don't like themselves. They are people who also mistreat and disrespect themselves. There is nothing you could ever do to please someone who is like this. So don't waste your life crying over the rejection and disappointment they brought you. Show kindness, hold your head up, and move on.

These people are distractions to your life journey, and you can stop them by not giving your valuable time and attention to them. Again, I cannot tell you how vitally important it is that you know who you are and know your value and worth. Unfortunately, people walk around with the behaviors I am talking about because they were unnurtured, unloved, and not emotionally supported as children. Be committed to yourself and committed to investing in yourself. You must take the focus off of other people and look solely at yourself. As you do this, make space in your daily routine to self-assess and reflect.

Self-assessment is necessary because you can see what you need to change. It may be difficult for you in the beginning, but the rewards of being honest with yourself will help you break free. You will break free from where you are to where you want to be. Get to a place of humility because humility will never lead you to focus on others' mistakes; it will always guide you to focus on your own.

Reflecting on yourself will help you identify what you have been doing that is counterproductive. Put into practice addressing others with love and boundaries. Love them where they are, and don't try to change them because the only person you are responsible for changing is you. It is important to set healthy boundaries with everyone so you can live a quality life. If you fail to set boundaries with people, they will get all they can from you because you are letting them.

Rejoice

Manage your time well every day because your time is a gift. We all value a gift, and time is a valuable gift. Stewarding your time with wisdom is your responsibility. Your beliefs, perspective about life, how you live, and your attitude can impact your time. People who died prematurely did not accomplish the things they were created for because they didn't value their time. They took the time they had for granted. They did not improve themselves, nor did they grow their character. Having an attitude impacts your whole being. You and I must have a positive attitude because our attitude will also affect our relationships. We need people in our lives who are emotionally healthy. We can only experience success with people. Our success in life will be dependent upon the people we choose. Deep-seated anger, resentment, bitterness, and unforgiveness impact our attitude and prevent us from having good character. Complaining and grumbling will not move us into a victorious, successful life. These attitudes work against us, and we cannot grow or develop character with negativity. We only build character when we adjust our mindset and never forget that we are our worst enemy. I have learned from living that I am my own worst enemy! You are your own worst enemy! You are the only one with the power to stop you from success, good health, and a life of joy and peace. You must realize that you have that much control over your life, and that is why you are the one who is responsible for your outcome. I have been privileged to meet various types of people throughout my adult life.

People from different cultures, ethnicities, religions, and different socialization experiences. I love the diversity I experience in people, and I have fully embraced their diversity. What I cannot welcome is the idea of being like someone else. Many people struggle with being who they are. If everyone challenged themselves to get to know themselves, they would not try to be like others. There is much about ourselves to discover, but we must be willing to invest the time to find out who we are. You and I possess amazing gifts, abilities, talents, and strengths. Every person has them, and no one is lacking in any way. We all possess exciting qualities and uniqueness in our personality that represent who we are. It is unhealthy when you and I want to be like others. It harms you and me when others do not embrace us because we are not like them. Diversity offers the opportunity for individual growth. Diversity can bring you into expansion because it represents a larger picture. Diversity brings a vast view with variety. Variety can expand your perspective where you see beyond your experiences to many others. Diversity elevates our character when we embrace the differences in others. When you cannot embrace the diversity in another, their beliefs, perspective, and culture, you will harm them.

Don't be a disruptor to someone you don't understand because they are different from you. Instead, treat them with value. Even if they don't look like you, talk like you, or live like you do.

Rejoice

We are who we are and what we have lived based on our socialization and beliefs. Be open to diversity, and you will expand yourself to being an exceptional human being. Remember, we all have value no matter who we are, where we have been, or what we have done. We are imperfect human beings, and our imperfections often require adjustments to our attitude. We should get to where we benefit others, not cause them to stumble. We must understand that people are purposefully in our lives, and what we give them in words and actions comes back to us. If you think about your attitude this way, it allows you to consider showing up in a better way. We must understand whatever we want from others should be what we reciprocate. Now, let me interject this thought and understanding to you. Your home environment influences what you do. However, what happened to you as a child is not an excuse for your poor attitude. You have the power to change that, and only you can change your mindset. The road you want to travel is the road to maturity and success. Remember, mature people are successful people. Successful people do not blame others or make them responsible for what they do and say! You must steward your life, owning your decisions, mistakes, and how you use your resources. Your words, your choices, and your actions shape your life. You are the one who is accountable for what you experience. You and only you! You cannot expect to be successful looking at what someone else should have done or didn't do.

These things are distractions to your joy, health, wealth, and success! If you want to live happy, fulfilled, and at peace, remember that your investment must begin with you first! Your gift of time is your time to give to you. Now is the time to build your mind, spirit, body, emotions, and life, which will put you in the direction of success. Success is living well and living out your capabilities, those things you can do. Know yourself, and not just your strengths but your weaknesses, too. Everything starts with you! If you are not doing anything to help yourself be who you are supposed to be, how can anyone truly help you? Everything begins with you!

Think about how you treat other people. Now, think about how you treat yourself. I seek to be kind towards others because I want kindness to return to me. However, I am not always kind to myself. I plan to eat a healthy meal, but a phone call interrupts with the voice on the other end saying help. The proper response would be to tell the individual you are unavailable then. Think about how you could help yourself at that moment without compromising the kindness you need to give to yourself. The best way to handle a phone call or anything else is not to answer. Don't answer the phone when doing something you need to do for yourself. Eating is a part of our lives, but we take eating for granted, like many other things. The way that we eat a meal impacts our bodies negatively or positively.

Medical issues develop because we eat quickly or eat unhealthy foods. I used eating as an example, but another example is getting enough sleep to maintain good health.

These examples of being kind to yourself are common sense. However, what we learn as children determines whether we will be kind to ourselves as adults. For many of us, our childhood experiences introduced us to repetitive, unkind acts. Everything we see and hear as children becomes part of our life experiences. Then, we grow up doing those cruel things we saw and heard to ourselves, keeping the cycle of abuse active. If you were never nurtured as a child and never received emotional support, do not let it be your song. Understand that you and I do not have to believe whatever was said and done. You can nurture yourself and build a robust support system around your life with those who can help you. Keep your heart open to learn what you never knew about kindness and how it is essential for you to give to yourself. There are many things you can do to show yourself compassion. One vital thing for every human being is to be loved, embraced, and accepted. Give yourself love, and embrace yourself because you are worthy of love. Never believe the unkind things people told you when you were a child. You have to do some work on this one. Words are powerful and crushing to a soul. If you need help, ask for help. You can seek the support of others to help you manage and address the painful things you have experienced.

Shut the tapes off playing in your subconscious mind and build yourself up daily with positive words affirming you. Meditation will assist you in producing change as you speak positive words to yourself.

You cannot afford to continue to live your life through someone else's wrong view of you. You can take these steps to change direction and get on the path to success. Change your thinking through the word of God by meditating on it. It is your thinking that you must change to experience a fulfilling life.

> Romans 12:2 (ERV) Don't change yourselves to be like the people of this world, but let God change you inside with a new way of thinking. Then you will be able to understand and accept what God wants for you. You will be able to know what is good and pleasing to him and what is perfect.

> Romans 8:5-6 (NLT) Those who are dominated by the sinful nature think about sinful things, but those who are controlled by the Holy Spirit think about things that please the Spirit. So letting your sinful nature control your mind leads to death. But letting the Spirit control your mind leads to life and peace.

Rejoice

Philippians 4:8 (AMP) Finally, believers, whatever is true, whatever is honorable and worthy of respect, whatever is right and confirmed by God's word, whatever is pure and wholesome, whatever is lovely and brings peace, whatever is admirable and of good repute; if there is any excellence, if there is anything worthy of praise, think continually on these things [center your mind on them, and implant them in your heart].

Job 22:21, 28 (NLT) Submit to God, and you will have peace; then things will go well for you. You will succeed in whatever you choose to do, and light will shine on the road ahead of you.

Psalms 34:11-16 (TPT) Come, children of God, and listen to me. I'll share the lesson I've learned of fearing the Lord: Do you want to live a long, good life, enjoying the beauty that fills each day? Then never speak a lie or allow wicked words to come from your mouth. Keep turning your back on every sin, and make "peace" your life motto. Practice being at peace with everyone. The Lord sees all we do; he watches over his friends day and night. His godly ones receive the answers they seek whenever they cry out to him. But the Lord has made up his mind to oppose evildoers and to wipe out even the memory of them from the face of the earth.

Everything Starts With You

1 Peter 2:2-3 (TPT) *In the same way that nursing infants cry for milk, you must intensely crave the pure spiritual milk of God's Word. For this "milk" will cause you to grow into maturity, fully nourished and strong for life — especially now that you have had a taste of the goodness of Yahweh and have experienced his kindness.*

Isaiah 43:18-19 (ERV) *So, don't remember what happened in earlier times. Don't think about what happened a long time ago, because I am doing something new! Now you will grow like a new plant. Surely you know this is true. I will even make a road in the desert, and rivers will flow through that dry land.*

Chapter 4
Supernatural Encounters

2019 was a transition year for me. As I moved through the year, I decided to move in a new direction. I wanted to be more intentional in my actions and words. My Mom had passed away. I wondered how I would keep her memory alive. I thought I had better not let sorrow and grief grab me. One month after her funeral, I had a spiritual encounter. Inside me, I heard I don't have to grieve if I don't want to. This dialogue inside of me continued. I heard in my heart that I will give you beauty for your ashes, joy for the sorrow you feel, and a spirit of praise for the heaviness you are carrying in your heart. I was hearing the voice of God's Spirit speaking to me. The Holy Spirit spoke words from the scripture in Isaiah Chapter 61, verse three, to my heart. My emotions rose, and I thought, "Yeah, I don't have to grieve or be sad. It is my choice." The heaviness I felt was walking with my mom through her storm and remembering her desire to live yet knowing she was dying. Those words I heard one month after her death moved me in a better direction.

I let go of the heaviness and the sadness and embraced peace. Then we entered 2020, and a close family member who honored my mom's request to sing at her funeral service passed away. I traveled home in March 2020 to show my love and respect and returned from travel to learn we were in a pandemic worldwide. I began to spiral quickly in my physical health, not knowing for sure what was happening in my body, but whatever it was, it had started to create a lot of issues. In the middle of 2020, I began experiencing emotional stress that elevated to the point that I didn't know if I was going to recover. Suddenly, I had an experience I will describe as a supernatural encounter. In this encounter, it felt like someone had removed a large blanket from my mind. I saw two colors, pink and yellow. I got up to transform the private space of my bedroom with these two colors. I immediately purchased yellow curtains, a large yellow square area rug, and a large round blush pink rug. I also purchased pink and yellow bed linens. This encounter showed me that it is about changing my view from all the ugly to seeing what is beautiful. My focus had shifted, and my motivation became a search for pink and yellow clothing. I began to choose to see through a different lens, which was vital to my emotional health. Then, I saw a vast field of yellow roses with blush pink butterflies alighting each rose. What a spectacular sight to see, and I felt myself beginning to come out of the thing that had gripped me into a place of emotional breaking. I was experiencing what felt like healing.

There was a notable shift in my mind as I surrounded myself with these two uplifting colors. I became overwhelmed with a strong sense of hope. I remember joy flooding my heart. The joy I experienced was attached to the vision I have been carrying for years.

If you know anything about vision, it is progressive. My vision was developing and had taken a new face, representing joy and peace, while my previous logo was representative of sorrow and pain. My heart knew the yellow rose with the blush pink butterfly alighting it was my new logo. It was original yet different and representative of where my vision was going! At that time, I didn't see the whole picture, but a peaceful and uplifting change occurred. During the progression of my vision's logo in July 2020, I entered a local Staples store to get business cards printed. It only took the young lady who served me a few minutes to print my business cards with a yellow rose and a blush pink butterfly alighting the rose. She was the right person and effortlessly executed my request. It was a fantastic experience, and it felt like she was waiting for me to show up to assist. God is so intentional. The young lady's name was Sunny, and she was very courteous, friendly, and knowledgeable. On August 21, 2020, I awakened with the word Rejoice in my heart and thoughts. There was so much joy in my heart when I awakened that morning. I had yet another supernatural experience because August 21st was my mom's birthday. This encounter with the word Rejoice was like I had to celebrate even though my mom was no longer here.

Rejoice

I had a steady flow of thoughts as I began to write an encouraging message entitled Rejoice. The word Rejoice continued to come to me. It had become a part of my focus, but I only realized it at the end of 2022. In December 2022, I had been focusing on and studying the book of Philippians in the bible, specifically chapter 4. Philippians chapter 4 was a letter written by the incarcerated man, Paul, which I mentioned in the first chapter. He was talking about rejoicing and what should be in our thoughts. While reading chapter 4 of the book of Philippians, I received a card during Christmas in 2022 from one of my Mom's high school classmates. I had met this lady for the first time during my Mom's celebration of life service. I was left wondering how this lady got my address because I did not get an opportunity to give it to her at my mom's funeral. It seemed unusual to me because she was contacting me for the first time after my Mom had passed three years prior. The card she sent me was beautiful. Amazingly, the card contained the word Rejoice on the front of it. The front of the card also included one of the two scriptures I had been studying in chapter 4 of the book of Philippians. A woman was in the dance posture on the front of the card. Then, a few days after receiving this, I went into the closet in my bedroom and pulled out my giant box of cards. I had no idea why I was rummaging through the box full of cards. To my surprise, a Christmas card with the word Rejoice on the front was in the box. There were also three angels on the front of the card. When I opened the card, there was no signature or personal writing.

Amazingly, I could not recall where this card came from, when I received it, or who sent it. I noticed on the back of this card that I had found in my card box that the card my Mom's friend had sent me was from the same company. So here I am in December 2022 with two cards containing Rejoice on the front and the Rejoice message I wrote in 2020 on my deceased mom's birthday. I do not believe in coincidence, and I know nothing just happens.

Everything happens for a purpose or reason. Towards the end of December 2022, I heard the words Rejoice and Focus in my heart, knowing I was to live these two words out in 2023. January 8, 2023, those two words I heard and saw in December 2022 were before me again. My Pastor invited an Apostle to come in and minister to our congregation. He came in and taught from the book of Philippians, and his text of scripture was Philippians Chapter 4, beginning at verse 4 and then to verse 8. He spoke Rejoice and Focus using the word fix instead of the word focus. The supernatural power of God had intercepted my focus through the book of Philippians in which I was meditating. At the beginning of 2023, I understood that God wanted me to write a book entitled Rejoice. I thought this would be a quick writing, but as 2023 unfolded, I realized this book was experiential. As a result, some of my encounters are in the pages of Rejoice. Last January, I remember pondering on the life of the incarcerated man who wrote a letter to the world telling us to rejoice.

Rejoice

He told us to fix or focus our thoughts on things that are lovely, just, true, honest, pure, and of a good report. My experience with his letter has inspired me to continue to move in the direction of joy. My thoughts, my mind, and my life have aligned with these words he wrote. I don't know about you, but it is clear that he gave us a key to win in adverse circumstances. Our focus must be positive if we intend to win in our trials. So, what are you focused on? What has your attention right now? Is it an unfavorable report? Is it the latest news report? Is it the report of poor health? It could be the negative thoughts swirling around in your mind. Your mind is the gateway to you. A mind that is busy, distracted, and cluttered is unhealthy. An unhealthy mind then results in a sick body. Everything about you is connected. Your mind is the part of you that soaks up your experiences, encounters, and events in your life. It is the part of you that will put the events of your life on replay. These events become a part of your thoughts when they are on replay, and then you speak them out loud into your atmosphere. You are creating your world through your mind, thoughts, and words. Your focus is one of the most important aspects of your life. You may have experienced physical and emotional issues as I did during the pandemic, but let us shift our focus. Let our focus be positive no matter what happens. Our takeaway from the pandemic should be gratitude, with our focus on the fact that we are still here. Meditate on positive things and only welcome positive thoughts. Let us fix our minds on these words. I am coming out on top.

I am strong in God and His mighty power. He is with me and will be with me as He was with Moses. Nothing and no one will ever be able to stop me from living in triumph. I am victorious and prosperous. As I cultivate more love in my heart, fear will not thrive in me. Love lives in me. The love in me throws out any fear. God has not given me fear.

He has given me the presence of the Holy Spirit, the Spirit of love and power. The Holy Spirit helps me to have self-control. I have control over myself, and my mind is sound. Let us receive His powerful love that transforms, heals, and liberates us.

If you are limited in love, you should familiarize yourself with Paul's New Testament writing in his letter to the Corinthian church. In 1 Corinthians Chapter 13, Paul's writing expounds on what God's love is. Without love, you cannot have faith; without faith, you cannot stand against fear. Where there is no love, there is no faith. We need love to operate our faith well and to stand against fear. We need God's love to battle fear when it comes. Fear immobilizes you and torments you in the area of your mind where it wants to gain access. If you have experienced trauma, you must deal with it because it produces fear in our hearts. In February 2023, during my prayer time, I asked the Holy Spirit two significant questions. The first question was: What is it that I believe about me? The second question was: What negative words are playing in my subconscious mind?

Rejoice

Then, in May 2023, I asked the Holy Spirit three more questions during one of my prayer times. The first question was: What in the natural realm keeps me stressed? The second question was: What behaviors am I displaying as a result of trauma? The third question was: What is in my life that causes me to draw toxic, abusive people? I needed to ask myself these hard questions because of some things I had experienced. I want to be the best I can be, so I know I must be honest with myself. You will need to do the same to live a life full of joy. The Holy Spirit did respond to my questions. I decided to speak to the negativity speaking to me. I started building a fortress of powerful, positive words over myself, affirming myself. It works! Speaking uplifting words to empower yourself is a spiritual exercise. Establishing yourself with positive words reinforces your heart. In July 2020, my sight shifted, which helped me move from negativity to positivity. Think about things that are lovely, just, true, honest, pure, and of an excellent report. If you do these things, you will rise above whatever tries to knock you down and soar.

> *Isaiah 61:3* (KJV) *to appoint unto them that mourn in Zion, to give unto them beauty for ashes, the oil of joy for mourning, the garment of praise for the spirit of heaviness; that they might be called trees of righteousness, the planting of the Lord, that he might be glorified.*

Supernatural Encounters

Philippians 4:4 (NLT) Always be full of joy in the Lord. I say it again—rejoice! And now, dear brothers and sisters, one final thing. Fix your thoughts on what is true, and honorable, and right, and pure, and lovely, and admirable. Think about things that are excellent and worthy of praise.

1 Corinthians 13:4-7 (AMP) Love endures with patience and serenity, love is kind and thoughtful, and is not jealous or envious; love does not brag and is not proud or arrogant. It is not rude; it is not self-seeking, it is not provoked [nor overly sensitive and easily angered]; it does not take into account a wrong endured. It does not rejoice at injustice, but rejoices with the truth [when right and truth prevail]. Love bears all things [regardless of what comes], believes all things [looking for the best in each one], hopes all things [remaining steadfast during difficult times], endures all things [without weakening].

Chapter 5

The Love Factor

Love: nothing is more significant than real love. Love is the center of where your life begins. Love should be what guides you in your daily routine, your decisions, your thoughts, and your heart. Without real love, you will not prosper. Love is the essence of your life, and Love made you for love and to love. God created you to experience real love. That is why every human being wants to be loved and accepted! Love is something we all fight for. Is this because everyone is challenged by how they treat themselves? Do you love yourself? Do you have love for others? If you do not love yourself, you cannot love another person. If you do not treat yourself with value, you will not value others. How do you see yourself? If you do not see the great things in you, you will not see the great things in others. Love is about being kind to yourself and seeing your value and worth. Then, you can show others kindness, showing them value and worth. Do you know that what you are is what you attract? So, if you are an unhappy, mean-spirited person, this will be the kind of people you will attract to yourself.

Knowing this is vital to changing your self-image and how you see yourself.

You are worthy of love and worth receiving love from another human being. One of the most incredible displays of real love is someone, a stranger, putting themselves in harm's way to protect an innocent baby or a pregnant woman. That is the ultimate act of love. The one willing to risk their life to save another knows real love. Jesus Christ came into this world and risked His life for you and me. He was sent into this world by God, Almighty, to die and give up His life for every human being. The love He has for us all is authentic. Every person who believes that Jesus is the Son of God and has accepted Him personally in their hearts through confession from their mouth possesses this kind of love within. This love is in the heart of every believer. Every day, we are supposed to give this love to everyone around us. However, we must yield to God's Spirit to develop this love within us. We must be willing to surrender to this love we carry and die daily to ourselves. Jesus died the ultimate death for us all, and as His followers, we are to die daily to our selfish desires. This love looks like showing patience and kindness to others and putting them above yourself. When you love like God, you choose peace instead of being argumentative. You will be the first to apologize even if you didn't create the problem. You will not tear other people down with your mouth. Your focus will be on being a better you. God's love inspires us to be the answer to someone else's needs.

The Love Factor

Real, authentic love is not an emotion but a force that remains loyal and doesn't quit. Love heals and restores others. Real love is the kind of love that embraces, is compassionate, sacrificial, robust, courageous, and everlasting, and has power over fear.

Fearful people cannot love others. People driven by fear have hearts full of jealousy, envy, pride, and other evil behaviors. We must live with boundaries as we interact with others and even ourselves. If you set no limits with yourself, you will not set boundaries with others. Boundaries are necessary because having boundaries places parameters around your life that will benefit you. I have set a limit to refrain from purchasing sugary, high-calorie foods. I will not eat it if I don't buy it and bring it home. Another boundary I have set is driving past a Krispy Kreme donut shop and not stopping. Yes, I love sugar and donuts, but I love myself more. These examples of boundaries I have set for myself have protected me from what is not suitable for me. Now, think about yourself. Ask yourself what limits have you set for you. If you can't think of any, this would be the opportune moment to make some space for yourself to assess the value you hold for yourself. Right now is the suitable time because there is no time in a day that you should waste. From my life journey, the absence of self-love contributed to my poor living. As a younger woman, my lifestyle was without restraint and control. I ate a lot of junk foods high in sugar daily. I lived a lifestyle without restrictions, doing things that were unhealthy.

Rejoice

You can harm yourself more than anyone else if you don't have a genuine love for yourself. Get some space between your daily routine and get alone with you. Write down your daily routine to see how you plan your day on paper. If your daily decisions are harmful, then ask yourself some hard questions. Such as, "Why don't I love myself?" Why do I do things that I know are bad for me? What am I willing to do to change this? After asking yourself these questions, answer honestly. Seek a mental health professional if you struggle to make a positive change. You may have some unresolved trauma. Unresolved trauma shows up in unhealthy habits, vices, and behavior. Repeated traumatic events can cause a person to be self-destructive. Indeed, this was an issue for me. I can quickly and easily detect self-destructive behaviors in others. Those who tend to behave this way suffer from rejection and emotional abuse. Life is unenjoyable for the self-destructive person. When someone comes along that can bring joy to their lives, they cannot sustain a healthy relationship because they live in the repetitive behavior of self-harm. Love for yourself is vital to living well and loving others. Unresolved repeated trauma also manifests in a person inflicting physical and emotional harm towards others. The person who lives with this behavior is acting out what they have experienced. Again, seeking professional counseling is necessary for any person who has experienced repeated trauma. You may have difficulty doing the right things for yourself. Your tendency to fall short may be due to you internalizing the trauma as something you deserved.

Maybe you have difficulty maintaining consistency. Consistency is a key to successful living and a significant part of a joy-filled life. God's love enveloping your heart is the most powerful of all. His amazing love for you can bring you to loving yourself.

Some years ago, I experienced the tangible presence of God's love. This experience happened while I was at church. As a result of this experience, I understand the heart of God and His desire that we love ourselves.

I have chosen to love myself regardless of whether anyone else does; however, loving myself did not happen overnight. It has taken me many years to embrace the love for me that God gave me. God's love gives me the ability to love others. Sharing my life with you is my love for you. I want you to make it. I want to provide you with hope because with hope comes expectation, and with expectation comes what you hope and desire. Let me take a moment to share what expectations are. You can want something, but until you expect it, you will not receive it. Expectation is on the same playing field as faith, but expectation does not come before faith. You cannot get something you desire without faith because faith believes. Faith is believing something can happen even though you cannot see it. You must have faith to believe, and then you can expect what you believe to happen. So have faith and have expectations. Do you realize the significance of your life? The world needs what is inside of you.

Rejoice

Your contribution is significant to people you still need to meet. If you don't do good things for yourself in your daily routine, why are you doing something to benefit others? Think about it. What is your reason for being committed to helping others but having no commitment to yourself? Is it that you have a need in you that's driving you to help others? Do you have an internal belief that doing what you do for them will get them to fix your needs? Or is what you do for them motivated by your desire to be liked and pleasing to them? Friend, if this is you, consider this an issue of unrealistic expectations. No one can fix you or your needs but you. The people you help should not expect you to fix their needs when they are responsible for their own lives and needs. You are responsible for your life and your needs. You have to develop love for yourself. My spiritual life was what helped me develop a love for myself. Having a spiritual life is another tool that can help you get free. Get free from whatever has happened in your life that keeps you from seeing your value and worth. Genuine love for yourself is the kickstarter and hinges on whether you live your best life. Stop the busy hustle-bustle mindset you have. Daily, you wrestle with getting up and doing 20,000 things with a long to-do list, a list with everybody you know on it except for yourself.

You have created this routine and let others influence how you spend your day. You are doing more harm to yourself than others could ever do because you don't see you. You must see yourself.

The Love Factor

Real Love is seeing you, what is good for you, and what you need. I can talk about this because this was me. What I know about myself is that I am compassionate, and I don't want anyone to be in need. I am an empathetic woman. I love people! What do you know about yourself? Write that down also when you write down your daily routine. I have lived only seeing people and never seeing myself for most of my life. The moment I saw myself and what I needed, I could see what I didn't need to give to people. I need time to be in the moment, enjoy the beauty, and feel the love around me.

Like myself, you need the time to enjoy the moment, the beauty all around you, and the love surrounding your life. Look around and see that Love is everywhere. Love is in the cool breeze on a hot summer day. Love is in the laughter of children playing in the park. Love is in the sound of birds singing loudly.

Love is in the smile of a baby. Love is in the country field of yellow roses. Love is in the crashing waves of the ocean. Love is in the starry sky. Love is in the warm rays of the sun! Love is at the dawn of a new day. Love is in every exhale and inhale of the breath you and I take. Love kisses you and me every morning, awakening us. Love is in the song inside your heart. Love is in every one of your steps. Love is even in every dark place and every dark space. Love is life! Love is power! Love is in a warm embrace! Love is giving kindness to those in pain.

Love is embracing what is unwanted and unloved. Love is you, and love is me. Love is something every human being desires and needs. Everyone is looking for someone to see that they need to be loved. You are the love that someone else needs. You were made for love and made to love. Have you ever been touched by real Love? Real Love is the love that doesn't remind you of your mistakes. If you have ever known real Love, you can distinguish it from what is fake. Real Love motivates you to love even when it is undeserved. If you plant this love into your surroundings and others, you will bring it back to you. Love is a force.

Love can take the most savage and tame that heart to that of a peaceful human being. Many years ago, I met a lady who was angry, disrespectful to authority, and rebellious. God guided me to make peace with this lady by addressing her, not her behavior. What I did not know then was how talking to her, not at her, and listening to what she had to say would spark a remarkable change in her. This lady was operating by the negative thoughts swirling in her mind, which was the culprit producing her disrespectful behavior. I am so glad I followed God's lead with her because she was never the same after that conversation. She needed to share the pain she was carrying. She needed someone to understand and listen. When I was younger, I met a lady who loved me every day for a year and a half. We were strangers, but she was no stranger to love. I had never been treated so kindly before meeting her. I received her kindness.

The love she demonstrated in action changed me. I was experiencing genuine love, the kind of Love that didn't have any conditions. I was free to be still who I was, a hurting, angry, bitter young woman, and that love she was carrying still wanted me.

Do you understand why I say that love is powerful? This real love extended to me has been a guidepost throughout my life and spiritual journey. This encounter with love would later pour into the life of the woman I talked about earlier. The seed of love deposited in me years earlier was not just for me. It blessed me to know I had planted the same seed of love I received into the lady whose heart was full of anger and disrespect. When one human being chooses to give real love to another human being, that person is aware of the language of the universe. Love is all around. Love is the language of the universe.

You and I can provide others with a superficial love, or we can give them a love that embraces them where they are. As I have lived my life, I have realized many people do not have a love for themselves. I have encountered many people, especially women, who did not authentically love themselves for who they are.

People who lack self-love cannot love others. You cannot give something that you do not have. It is difficult for an unnurtured person to love themselves.

Rejoice

What is in people is what they offer. Many women resort to jealousy, unkindness, competitiveness, envy, comparison, manipulation, control, and divisiveness. These behaviors come from the traumatic and negative experiences they were impacted by as children. Even though the traumatic experiences have ended, unresolved trauma will remain with that person until there is a resolution of the trauma. Many people, both men and women, have experienced rejection, abuse, violence, abandonment, and a lack of emotional love as children. It is essential to be sensitive to the needs of others and whatever they lack. You consider them despite their behavior because you understand they need the love that can free them. You know that love is something you give, not because someone deserves it. You understand that love is a universal basic need of every human being. Whether they have received it or not, it is still a need. We are responsible for giving to people what we sense all around us. The beauty we see in creation is an expression of love. Creation speaks differently from us, but creation still speaks. It is never saying we don't have the right to enjoy it, but it says we can. Just like love speaks to us. Love doesn't say we don't have the right to receive it. Love just gives us the love we need. We want to do the same for people. We should love people not because they deserve it but because we can give love. What kind of world would this be if we let the love of the Messiah, the Christ, the Savior, King, and Lord of all sustain us physically and emotionally?

The Love Factor

What would this world be like if we chose to love unconditionally? Jesus loves us so much that He was willing to die a gruesome death to put every human being in a position to enter freely into the presence of an Almighty God! His death was a display of genuine sacrificial love. Living a love life begins with you loving you. Take the time you have and start your journey of love. Get your time back because you are not here forever. It is to your advantage to save time, not waste it. Do not take this gift you have for granted. Finally, having genuine love for yourself is the posture for experiencing joy. You cannot have joy in your heart if you do not have love in your heart. Joy is something we can all share when we have genuine love living in our hearts. Love begins in you. Live the journey of love for yourself, and joy will come. Then you will live strong because that joy in you will produce strength. Establish a positive daily routine to center your thoughts in a positive place.

Focus on your strengths every day and study your weaknesses. Speak your strengths aloud every day to build yourself. Meditating on your strengths helps you develop a healthy view of yourself. The way you see yourself is vital to what you accomplish. Study your weaknesses to identify what you need to change.

Challenge yourself to change the shortcomings you discover. If you need more patience, go to the store early to avoid large grocery lines.

Rejoice

Don't worry about developing patience because there will be many things in your life that will teach you patience.

Applying spiritual and natural wisdom will help you locate where and who you are. You are loved, unique, incredibly beautiful, and valuable! Affirming you is the spark to develop a genuine love for yourself. Remember, you must love yourself to love another because you cannot do one without the other.

> *1 John 4:16* (CSB) *And we have come to know and to believe the love that God has for us. God is love, and the one who remains in love remains in God, and God remains in him.*
>
> *John 3:16* (ERV) *Yes, God loved the world so much that he gave his only Son, so that everyone who believes in him would not be lost but have eternal life.*
>
> *Mark 12:30-31* (AMPC) *And you shall love the Lord your God out of and with your whole heart and out of and with all your soul (your life) and out of and with all your mind (with your faculty of thought and your moral understanding) and out of and with all your strength. This is the first and principal commandment. [Deut. 6:4, 5.] [31] The second is like it and is this, You shall love your neighbor as yourself. There is no other commandment greater than these. [Lev. 19:18.]*

The Love Factor

1 Corinthians 13:13 (AMP) *And now there remain: faith [abiding trust in God and His promises], hope [confident expectation of eternal salvation], love [unselfish love for others growing out of God's love for me], these three [the choicest graces]; but the greatest of these is love.*

John 15:9-10 (TPT) *I love each of you with the same love that the Father loves me. You must continually let my love nourish your hearts. If you keep my commands, you will live in my love, just as I have kept my Father's commands, for I continually live nourished and empowered by his love. My purpose for telling you these things is so that the joy I experience will fill your hearts with overflowing gladness!*

Chapter 6

A Prophetic Insight of Seasons

Have you looked at your life lately? Do you realize that everything you have experienced has been just for a season? All the seasons we enter have a specific purpose for our lives. Seasons come with assignments. You must know the season or appointed time you are in because it helps you to identify the assignment attached to that season. I would never have known my assignment in the seasons of my life without a personal relationship with God, and neither will you. God knows why He created you. For example, when I entered school to secure my spiritual education, this appointed time carried an assignment. The assignment was to capture the vision I was unaware of in my heart. That vision was revealed to me during this specified time through two scriptures. John 17 and Isaiah 61:1-3 stood out as I studied God's word during this season. These words grabbed me to the degree that I acknowledged them verbally daily.

My heart connected with God's word, and His word unveiled my assignment and vision. If I had not shifted to the season of transition and change, I may not have discovered what I was carrying. From that appointed time to this present time, I have continued to attend to the vision in me.

Do you know what season you are in? Do you know the personal seasons of your life? What is your vision, and what is your assignment? Know the seasons of your life because they are attached to appointed times. Seasons are appointments and periods where things happen according to that specific time. The four seasons require us to be strategic and ready to execute what we set in motion to experience our harvest and then prepare to shift to begin the cycle of seasons again. We start in a strategic season that moves us into an executing season, leading us into a harvesting season that ends in a shifting season. We must understand that our lives constantly operate in seasons. Moving too quickly in a season can cause us to lose something. Even worse, we could gain something that should never be in our lives. We must identify our seasons and live according to that present season. In the book of Ecclesiastes 3:1-8 (GNT), Remember everything that happens in this world happens at the time God chooses. He sets the time for birth and the time for death, the time for planting and the time for pulling up, the time for killing and the time for healing, the time for tearing down and the time for building.

A Prophetic Insight of Seasons

He sets the time for sorrow and the time for joy, the time for mourning and the time for dancing, the time for making love and the time for not making love, the time for kissing and the time for not kissing. He sets the time for finding and the time for losing, the time for saving and the time for throwing away, the time for tearing and the time for mending, the time for silence and the time for talk.

He sets the time for love and the time for hate, the time for war and the time for peace. All these things will happen at the time God has appointed. There is no way around birth and death, love and hate, planting and uprooting. These things must happen because God has established them. The book of Ecclesiastes reveals a strategy. Most people live the seasons of their lives based on what someone else has said or done. Within the seasons, a pattern and rhythm are present governing our lives. We all must access and apply that pattern and rhythm to our lives to have fruitfulness and strength in difficult seasons. Knowing the season you are in and living your life within the parameters of that season will keep you from things you do not need to experience.

For example, you receive an invitation to go somewhere and participate in an event. Your excitement begins to lead you into this venture. However, if you do not examine yourself to determine why you accept the offer, you may be setting yourself up for moving prematurely. Always be in the right place at the right time.

Rejoice

Timing is everything with God, and the timing for something lies within a season. You and I must implement a strategy with each season we enter. It is wise to live your life with strategies. Premature death can happen because you were doing something or went someplace out of the timing or season. It was not the season for you to plant the idea God gave you. It was not the season or appointed time to go west when you are in the season for traveling east. We must know the planting season and when the season becomes a harvest season. If you want to live a life of joy, apply the instructions of God's word, the Bible, and He will give you a strategy for every season of your life. Our lives align within the spectrum of the four seasons: winter, spring, summer, and fall. These four seasons are appointments in our lives that carry a purpose. Although seasons are natural, they have a connection to our spiritual life. That is why we must understand what each season represents. The winter season is a Strategic time. During this appointment of rest, we should be positioning ourselves in preparation for the new year we are entering. The winter is a season of resting and meditating between December, January, and February. During this time, everything in nature visibly reflects a season of barrenness. One winter, I was walking in a local park praying and noticed that one of the trees never shed its leaves and was still green. It was unusual yet profound to see this tree like that. It reminds me of how we live in the seasons of our lives; sometimes, we don't recognize the seasons have changed.

We stay one way when it is time to shift to another direction, action, and place. Winter is an important season that is often viewed as an uncomfortable season because the weather becomes fiercely cold. It is all about perspective. Winter is a time to be still and reflect, not run and jump. You can see things you would have typically missed in a season of reflection and stillness.

Winter is a season for focus. You rest and focus, meditating in a time of quietness. It is a time to gain clarity and focus on what is ahead. Focus on what you want to produce, create, and bring forth in the upcoming year. Take this season to pursue consistent prayer, which is your strategy.

As you pray, you should write down your goals and commit yourself to your goals and God! Prayer will help facilitate your focus as you meditate and help you see what is not apparent. Prayer is a weapon! I have often thought that rest is a weapon. Take advantage of resting this season like the bear who goes into hibernation. Physical rest gives us the advantage because a well-rested body and mind operate optimally. When we enter spiritual rest, we place our complete trust in God. Entering spiritual rest allows God to work on your behalf because you are not trying to do things in your strength. You are trusting Him to do what you believe Him to do.

Rejoice

Death and loss occur in every season; however, the winter season brings the appointment of death and loss that is more impactive. Winter is the end of something. Tangible things all around us reflect this season of death and loss. Such as the leaves of a tree dying off and flowers losing their blooms. Birds fly to warmer climates because what they need is no longer available in this season. We should be wise enough to recognize our season has changed when what we need for survival is no longer available. In the winter season, we exit one year, an old season, to enter a new year, a new season. Like the birds, whatever we need in the old season is no longer available, and to survive, sometimes we must shift to another place. Everyone will not enter that new year because, within 365 days, we are moving between seasons that are appointed times. There is an appointed time to die and be born. We should facilitate the winter season with prayer, meditation, rest, and preparation. We must be ready to launch into the next season and exit this season strong. Leaving winter leads us into a season to plant those things we were giving attention to and reflecting on. Make this your time to set things in motion. As we move into the spring season, we enter into a time of execution. The spring is a planting and preparing season between March, April, and May. The Spring season is a season of sowing your plans and dreams. It is an exciting season because you are working to bring something from your heart to reality.

In this executing season, invest your time gathering and planting the right seeds at the right time to produce what you want. I want to think like a farmer as I talk about this season.

The farmer is responsible for planting good seeds into the soil to produce the crops he wants. There are three matters of importance here. First, the farmer must consider the condition of the seeds he will use. Are they the right seeds to sow? Secondly, is the quality of the seeds healthy enough to produce the harvest he desires? The third matter of importance is the soil condition and weather, which determines the best days to deposit the seeds. We must ensure what we sow is at the right time and is being deposited in the right place. This season is like the relationships we are planting into.

What do we bring forth while sowing in a relationship if we are sowing at the wrong time? Are these relationships good soil for us to plant in? Whatever we sow in this season will show up later. We can produce an unfavorable harvest if we sow into an unhealthy relationship.

Sometimes, we encounter people who are not those we should be sowing into because of the condition of their hearts. The soil of their heart is like the soil we plant seeds in to grow crops. If the soil is shallow, what we deposit will not take root. Since relationships are a large part of our lives, we should carefully inspect the soil.

Rejoice

We speak from our hearts when we communicate. Listen carefully to discern whether a person has an unhealthy heart. We should think like farmers in our relationships and want the soil to be pliable, not filled with rocks and debris. We should ensure the soil of people's hearts is malleable, especially those in close relationships. Are you specific about the kind of people you want to surround your life? I am carefully considering my relationships this season because I do not want an unhealthy harvest to appear in this new year. I do not want to set something in motion that will not produce life or start something that will not live. When I speak about a pliable heart, I am talking about someone not full of pride, arrogance, and criticism. It is challenging to plant love and kindness into the soil of a hard heart. Why? Trying to plant into stony soil is an emotional and physical struggle. Nothing can prosper or grow in rocky soil. Even a farmer will attest to this. You must determine whether the relationship is worth your emotional and physical effort. If so, be prepared to plow that stony heart with unconditional love. Planting the seed of love in the heart of any person makes it easy to water that heart. A heart filled with unconditional love can produce healing in other hearts. If you want springtime, let God's love make its home in your heart and inner self. It is our hearts that shape the seasons of our lives. His passionate love in us produces a never-ending life of beauty filled with peace and joy! Every season of our lives is vital because they interconnect with one another.

A Prophetic Insight of Seasons

The planting season is over, and we begin producing and harvesting what we planted. Summer is a flourishing producing season between June, July and August. The Summer is the appointed time to set what you planned from the previous season in motion. In this season, you can see what you have planted, and it is ready to go forth. We are in an active season involved with what we focused on, sowed, and prepared. This season, you can enjoy what you created if you planted at the right time and in the right conditions. Summer is a season of reaping your harvest and enjoying your labor. If you spent the spring season sowing negative words or a bad attitude, you should expect what you planted to show up in your summer. This season is a season of success or failure based on what you planted. What will you be harvesting? I can guarantee that whatever seed you deposited will flourish and grow. Previously, I mentioned a lady in another chapter, and I need to mention her again because it is relevant to this season. I spent a year and a half season with her, and it marked a new beginning for me. Her love and kindness set me on a different course in my life. I will never forget her.

Because of the season she was in, which was a planting season, her actions towards me brought a harvest.

Merlene consistently sowed love into me during the 548 days I encountered her. Five hundred forty-eight days later, she received a considerable harvest.

Rejoice

My life was met by God's love, resulting in my freedom. Those days with her remain a memorial because she loved me with her actions, not words. Genuine kindness that did not cost her anything to give. Her kindness motivated me to want to change. I want to ponder on this encounter for a moment. At that time in my life, I was not easy to love. I would not have made it if she had not decided to love me despite the anger, bitterness, and unforgiveness that I wore like a badge of honor. You may have met someone or know someone with a poor disposition. What if God has sent that person in your life for you to help rescue? After all, we are His hands and feet on the earth. Think about it this way and ask yourself these questions. Do I possess the God-kind of love that can transform another person's life? How many people will this person rescue after I help them? People need a rescue from themselves. My 548-day encounter was about rescuing me from myself and not just the pain I was carrying. Some people planted intentionally in our lives need a rescue from themselves. Were you created to change one person's life, whose purpose is to change many lives? What a powerful thought to consider. Discount no one in your life because every person is valuable regardless of who they are or what they have done. My rescue manifested in my decision to enter this lady's church on Sunday, April 29, 1986, where I said yes to Jesus Christ and welcomed Him into my heart and life. She brought me into a season of success as she planted something beautiful in me.

It was a season of success for me because my life was set in motion to go in a better direction. God is a God of seasons. He will constantly Shift us to something new, something unfamiliar, so we can continue to grow. When it is time to shift the things you once embraced, you stop accepting them because you have grown past them. God turned me from the pain I carried towards something new, a life of love that continues to grow me because I no longer accepted what hurt me. My journey began with me learning to love myself. Although seasons are temporary, loving myself is a forever venture.

No matter how brief our season is, there is always an appointed time flowing from one specific thing to another. There is always a shift, a transition happening. We exit the harvesting season to a season of Shifting. Everything starts to change when we enter the fall season. The Fall season is a time of changing and shifting between September, October and November. The Fall season is a season of transition and is the time we have to make adjustments like creation does all around us.

The trees become more vibrant in color. The leaves go from green to a bright shade of orange and red. Transition is not always comfortable; however, change must occur.

Sometimes, we have to shift to another place or job and exit from some relationships to new ones. Whatever your transition, understanding adjustments will help you get to the next season, which will be waiting for you.

Rejoice

Like the leaves changing color, we need to change direction from where we are to another position. This season reminds me of Vision. A vision does not become something else; it simply evolves like nature.

A vision has shape and within the seasons of appointed times that come, the vision transitions and changes just as the season changes. Your vision could represent sorrow and pain, but after the appointed time, the vision shifts to express joy and peace. As I reflect on this season of transition, my heart has changed. A transition took place. A shift happened, and I moved from mourning to dancing with a tangible experience of joy and peace. Everything that happens in this world happens at the time God chooses.

He lets us rest in fields of green grass, leads us to quiet pools of fresh water, and gives us new strength. God is always faithful, guiding us on the right paths, as promised. No matter what God chooses, He will always be with us to lead us and help us through each season.

> *Genesis 8:22 (GNT) "As long as the world exists, there will be a time for planting and a time for harvest. There will always be cold and heat, summer and winter, day and night."*

Psalms 30:11 (AMP) You have turned my mourning into dancing for me; You have taken off my sackcloth and clothed me with joy.

Ecclesiastes 3:1-8 (GNT) Everything that happens in this world happens at the time God chooses. He sets the time for birth and the time for death, the time for planting and the time for pulling up, the time for killing and the time for healing, the time for tearing down and the time for building. He sets the time for sorrow and the time for joy, the time for mourning and the time for dancing, the time for making love and the time for not making love, the time for kissing and the time for not kissing. He sets the time for finding and the time for losing, the time for saving and the time for throwing away, the time for tearing and the time for mending, the time for silence and the time for talk. He sets the time for love and the time for hate, the time for war and the time for peace.

Luke 8:15 (NLT) And the seeds that fell on the good soil represent honest, good-hearted people who hear God's word, cling to it, and patiently produce a huge harvest.

Hosea 11:4 (GNT) I drew them to me with affection and love. I picked them up and held them to my cheek; I bent down to them and fed them.

Rejoice

Psalm 23:2-3 (GNT) *He lets me rest in fields of green grass and leads me to quiet pools of fresh water. He gives me new strength. He guides me in the right paths, as he has promised.*

Chapter 7

Dance Partners

Dancing is powerful! It is a way to release something you do not need. Dancing has become my constant expression of joy! I enjoy the freedom it brings. I knew and understood as we entered into 2023 that I must choose to dance, laugh, sing, and Rejoice every day. As I stepped into the posture of joy, I was strong enough to overcome what would come in 2023. God knew I was going to enter a challenging season. While meditating on scripture, instruction was released in my heart to do two things: Rejoice and Focus. Throughout 2023, I danced to the rhythm of joy and peace no matter what happened. I was determined to choose the right dance partners. This decision moved me toward dancing daily because I spark joy when I dance. I danced at home, church, wedding receptions, and anywhere there was an opportunity to dance. I want the joy and peace in my heart to stay ignited! I even began to observe other people dancing, and seeing others laugh while they danced brought me great pleasure. Although I committed to dancing and Rejoicing at the beginning of 2023, the year brought a season of death.

Rejoice

The death of my father, who I loved, the death of relationships, and the death of those who positively impacted my life, yet death could not stop me from Rejoicing! I choose joy! I entered a posture of praise and worship to my God! I pushed past the sorrow, grief, and the pain of others' losses. I danced and laughed as if the deaths and losses had never occurred! How could I do this? I decided to celebrate in that season of sorrow and release joy.

I began to understand the seasons of our lives and how to navigate when they come. Good and bad seasons will come. If you and I celebrate now and make it a lifestyle, it will show up in our future. Let's plant seeds of joy now, so a year or five years down the road, we will be secure and sturdy in hard seasons. Make your time today count for your tomorrow. Spend time dancing, singing, and celebrating. It will change you. Joy is contagious and doesn't cost you anything. Imagine that you pay no money out of pocket to experience the freedom that heals you. Laughter will bring healing to your mind and body.

The Bible says that laughter is medicine. Our lives become healthier when we choose an upbeat attitude and express ourselves positively. What others will see when you decide to laugh is a person who is pleasant, friendly, content, confident, and happy. A happy heart is good medicine, and a joyful mind causes healing. Watch out! You may have to get rid of your medications messing with the power of joy.

Dance Partners

We generally think of one person as our dance partner but I have lived my journey with multiple dance partners. You may need more than one dance partner to make it through life. Who are you dancing with?

Do you dance with rejection and shame, or do you dance with fear and anger? I encourage you to change your dance partners so you can truly live. I have spent a lot of my life dancing with manipulative and harmful people. Are you dancing with negativity and toxicity in your associations with others?

You know, those people who manipulate and control you. You dance with an overestimation of others and an underestimation of yourself. You dance with negative communication from yourself and others. Negative people will block your ability to dance well. Are you the one who dances with pain and grief or maybe bitterness and shame? There was a time when I danced with rejection, fear, and anger, but today and for the rest of my life, I dance with love, joy, and peace. Some of us have learned to dance well alone, which is okay. But there are times when we need to have someone to dance with because dancing is a physical and emotional expression of intimacy. Dancing is expressing your emotional and physical self with someone else. When you choose to dance with someone, you are posturing yourself for intimacy. Intimacy is a building block in relationships; intimacy is the closeness we need.

There is vulnerability in dancing. Choosing to connect your physical and emotional expression to another can be uncomfortable. However, being vulnerable with others is essential for us to experience the freedom we need to live well. That's why dancing is so representative of freedom. Joy brings us to freedom because it breaks us from ourselves! Joy will make you strong enough to be bold and courageous! Imagine living your life restricted and sheltered with all your walls erected to keep everyone out. How can you live with joy when you have a fortress built around you? Your life is unfruitful and needs freedom from the silence and loneliness you surround yourself with.

Get an abundance of positive dance partners to bring fruitfulness to your life. Dancing with someone else will help you gain whatever you need. Because whatever you lack, someone else assuredly has what you need. To dance well, we learn from one another when to lead and when to follow. Dancing with another will require you to submit to their direction, and submitting to the person you dance with will likely result in them following your direction. We see this when people gather together to line dance. Line dancing is fun, healthy, and meaningful. It brings people together to move their bodies and emotions in a healthy direction. I have gained some new dance partners necessary for my fulfillment. I love dancing with boundaries, kindness, wisdom, compassion, and expectation. I have also learned to dance with others who were skillful in dance.

Dance Partners

People come into your life by divine providence to teach you how to dance well. My sister Sharon was one of those people. Sharon and I danced a lot at home and were brave enough to dance in public, often entering dance contests. Dancing was our hobby, and as far back as I can remember, my mom, Jenetta, danced throughout her life. To dance well, you must choose upbeat music that lifts your spirit. I know some people like to listen to music expressing sadness, loss, and sorrow, but this music will keep you stuck in a depressed state.

I love the upbeat contemporary gospel, and I like old-school rap music. Music can be like people. If you choose people who are always singing the blues, always expressing sorrow, sadness, and loss, you will never live joyfully.

So choose uplifting music and people who know how to live uplifting lives because both people and music release life or death, joy or sadness through their expression.

I miss dancing with my sister, and although she is no longer here, I am not without a dance partner. God knows who we need in our lives to get us into our next season. He knows how to bring the right people who can usher us to another level. He will intentionally choose people who will understand and accept you for who you are. People will come that you can trust and will demonstrate they are safe.

Rejoice

There is nothing like having a relationship with someone who cares about you. Love will bring you together. I am blessed to encounter a man whose heart is beautiful. The heart is vital for me because that is where everything begins. I have committed to establishing a meaningful relationship with him. We initially connected spiritually, and from that basis, we began establishing a friendship. He is valuable to me, and I respect him highly. As I get to know him, I see his imperfections but focus on his strengths. Why? I am not without weaknesses; besides, perfect people do not exist. I am growing my relationship with him without unrealistic expectations towards him. I accept him for the man he is. I understand that embracing him is vital to our thriving relationship. I extend to him what was once extended to me: love. Love embraces. The love in my heart is embracing him. I can dance through life with him, and I can grow in new ways because of the substance he carries. By the way, he thinks he can't dance, but he is a great dancer! Other people have seen us dance together and affirmed that we are both good dancers! As I dance with him, we are making an exchange. I let him lead the direction we move, and sometimes, I step in another direction for him to move with me. Dancing is like a relationship because an exchange happens when two people are willing to submit to their connection. This season of dancing I entered in 2023 that continues today has brought me into a new place! My life has experienced such a shift that I have moved beyond the old dance of past pain, and now I dance with my bright future.

The old dance is out, and the new dance is in! Will you eliminate the old dance of chaos and embrace peace as your partner? What about dancing with joy instead of sorrow or Love instead of fear? Love has the power to drive fear out of us and from us. Those things we were impacted by cannot override Love. Will you choose Love? Love is the way to success, joy, and peace. A hate-filled heart will not embrace joy and peace. Nor will a hate-filled heart be inspired to dance; however, hate always dances with fear. Hate and fear both oppose Love because they work to destroy. Love will lift you to live and empower you to stand against everything that opposes the Love in you. Love will let you see your value. Live like you have value because you do. Embracing yourself for who you are makes it easier to dance, sing, jump, shout, laugh, and stay joyful! Everyone and everything you encounter will respond to the joy you live in.

While you are rejoicing even in difficulty, others will not understand, but just keep on dancing anyway. Depression, sadness, and sorrow will not remain. The hard things will not keep your focus. Before you know it, you will have a different perspective.

The joyful flame burning in you will see the bad as an opportunity to expose what is dark to show the power of light. We can bring light to others whenever we overcome the dark in our lives. God is light, and His light will lead you into dancing.

Rejoice

He turned my mourning and crying into joyful dancing. I danced out of dark places into a space filled with light. He clothed me with joy! I danced out this past year with all the dark it brought and welcomed the new year with a contemporary dance. As this year unfolds, I dance with purpose! My praise is a weapon! My dance is a weapon against anything and everything that comes to restrict my joy and peace. I say goodbye to all the negative and hello to everything that elevates my heart and life. So let's dance! Young women dance for joy! Old and young men join in the celebration. For the Lord God says He will turn your mourning into joy. He will comfort you and exchange your sorrow for Rejoicing.

Proverbs 17:22 (AMP) *A happy heart is good medicine and a joyful mind causes healing. But a broken spirit dries up the bones.*

Psalms 30:11 (NLT) *You have turned my mourning into joyful dancing. You have taken away my clothes of mourning and clothed me with joy.*

Nehemiah 8:10 (AMPC) *And be not grieved and depressed, for the joy of the Lord is your strength and stronghold.*

Dance Partners

Nehemiah 8:10 (TLB) it is a time to celebrate with a hearty meal and to send presents to those in need, for the joy of the Lord is your strength. You must not be dejected and sad!"

1 John 4:18 (CSB) There is no fear in love; instead, perfect love drives out fear, because fear involves punishment. So the one who fears is not complete in love.

1 John 4:11-18 (MSG) God is love. When we take up permanent residence in a life of love, we live in God and God lives in us. This way, love has the run of the house, becomes at home and mature in us, so that we're free of worry on Judgment Day—our standing in the world is identical with Christ's. There is no room in love for fear. Well-formed love banishes fear. Since fear is crippling, a fearful life—fear of death, fear of judgment—is one not yet fully formed in love.

Jeremiah 31:13 (NLT) The young women will dance for joy, and the men—old and young—will join in the celebration. I will turn their mourning into joy. I will comfort them and exchange their sorrow for rejoicing.

Chapter 8

Weight Watchers

I want you to think about the times in your life when you felt overwhelmed and weighed down. You know what I am talking about. Those are the times you decide you would take on someone else's responsibility or when you decide to try to meet everyone else's needs. How is it working for you? You are caring and thoughtful because people who put others before themselves are. You're the person who meets others' needs and neglects your own. Can I tell you that you are setting yourself up to stumble, invite sickness, become physically overweight, and bring pressure you don't need? Trying to carry a weight can create pressure. I have held many weights throughout my life. Which means I have been chief at making poor decisions. My decision path was always choosing what was best for others. I have met many people who live this way. In observation, I noticed they were always stressed out and at the point of complaining. If you find yourself complaining, it is a sign you are living neglectful of your needs, and the pressure you feel from supporting others has increased.

Rejoice

If you never have time to eat or sleep, you are living in a self-destructive mode. Have you ever considered why you live this way? What I have discovered in reflection of my own life is that I have tried to live pleasing others. This behavior began early in my life. The childhood adversity I experienced inspired me to carry the weight of its impact. I found myself overweight in many areas until a significant event in my life inspired me to become a Weight Watcher. People pleasers can become overweight because those connected to their lives do not accept responsibility for their choices. Are you living under unnecessary stress? Do you often try to please others? If you have experienced rejection or unacceptance by others, do not live carrying this kind of pain. It will manifest in a behavior such as people pleasing or other undesirable learned behaviors. There are many learned behaviors that we display throughout our lives when there is unresolved trauma. No matter what you have experienced, you deserve respect and love. Address the negative impact of rejection and unacceptance so you can enjoy your life. Being a people pleaser can be exhausting. Imagine trying to please people who are never satisfied no matter what you do. If you are in this situation, I strongly suggest you shift.

Shift your life in another direction and get away from people who do not value the contribution you make towards them. Let me tell you that I have intentionally shifted my life so that peace is one of my dance partners. I dance with peace every day. I am a remarkable woman, one who lives in wisdom.

Weight Watchers

Let me tell you what has helped me shift to the way of life I live today.

Thirteen years ago, I suffered a brain trauma that required two doctors to work together to save my life. July 24, 2010, I was at home on a Saturday night, relaxing with my dog.

Suddenly, I had a pain in my head that felt like someone had a hammer hitting me with all their force. I stood up quickly and tried to put clothes on. I reached for my cell phone and called my Mom, telling her something was wrong. Then, I called all my children, beginning with my oldest son.

I instructed my oldest son to come and take me to the local hospital. It was getting late and was nearing 1100 pm. My oldest son got out of bed and arrived 25 minutes later. He drove me to the hospital, which was a 20-minute drive. I walked into the emergency room, declaring the pain in my head felt like someone was beating me with a hammer full force. It was a 45-minute wait in the emergency room before I received any medical care. When I heard my name called, I stood up. I remember standing up. As I got up from the chair, the aneurysm I was experiencing ruptured, and I slipped into an unconscious state. The emergency room staff quickly admitted me to the intensive care unit of the hospital. I intentionally shared the timeline of my receiving medical care because aneurysms are so deadly.

Rejoice

It amazes me that the aneurysm did not rupture within the first hour before I arrived at the hospital, and still, even almost an hour later, while sitting in the emergency room. I was in the hospital for fourteen days, with three of those days in the intensive care unit. Upon my initial assessment, a lady interventional radiologist determined I was experiencing an aneurysm. This doctor contacted another specialist in brain care to discuss how they would address my life-threatening situation. Both of my doctors deliberated for hours on the best course of action to save my life. At 100 pm on July 25th, the brain surgeon performed a 9-hour brain surgery, and titanium implants were placed in my head. The surgeon placed a large titanium plate in the front of my head, along with a 7 mm titanium clip inserted in my right eyebrow and two titanium screws in the top of my head to support my brain.

The doctors said they didn't know what condition I would be in nor if I would ever walk or talk. I have to pause for a moment on that statement. I want you to stay with me for a moment. Let's think about what I just shared. The doctors were able to save me from imminent death, but they didn't know if I could live well or have the ability to function as before. I suffered an aneurysm and a deadly hemorrhage to my brain. I also had hydrocephalus, which is water on the brain. Later, I experienced another life-threatening complication that the doctors were scrambling to address.

Despite the negative report the doctors gave my family, after 9 hours of working on my brain, I came out of surgery talking.

According to my family, I asked them three specific questions. God awakened me at 8:00 am on July 26, 2010, which was the day after my 9-hour brain surgery.

He began speaking these words to my heart, "Now we know all things work together for good to those who love God and to those who are called according to His purpose."

I responded, "Yes, Lord, I know that scripture." My brain surgeon walked into the room to assess me and was amazed to find me fully aware. I knew where I was, who I was, and what day of the week it was.

He scrambled out of the room to bring his parents in to meet me, the miracle as he had proclaimed. Again, I am remarkable, and indeed, I know I am a miracle.

What the doctors could not do that day, with confidence, I know that my God, Yahweh, was able to accomplish. I confidently tell you that no matter what we go through in our life journey, those circumstances work for us and not against us.

The God who created us is good. While He does allow bad things to happen, He is with us and keeps us through every circumstance.

Rejoice

If all hell has broken loose in your life and you didn't lose your mind, kill someone, or self-destruct, then God was with you. I can't explain why God allows evil to happen, but I can tell you that evil will work for you. It is like baking a cake; we know some ingredients are not good. However, those unpleasant ingredients are necessary for the cake. After you bake the cake, you cannot identify anything terrible in taste. You don't taste the baking soda or the eggs. You enjoy the cake because the flavor is sweet, not bitter or nasty. That is how it is with our lives as we live past the circumstances and adversities. When people see you, they do not know the pain you endured, the sorrow that overwhelmed you, or the trauma that gripped you. All they see is a beautiful, healthy, well-lit soul radiating love, joy, and peace. You must become a Weight Watcher to live an abundant life filled with joy and peace. When you think about weights, they can be cumbersome and difficult. But please understand the weights in this life are not ours to carry. When you take something heavy, it weighs you down. Those things that trouble your soul, like traumatic experiences, are heavyweights. Do you think you can carry those weights and expect to maintain good health and make good choices? Of course not. However, sometimes we have weights we don't know we are carrying. Maybe that's you. I discovered I had weights after I suffered my brain trauma. I recall eight months later pondering on what had happened to me. I was reasonably healthy at age 46 and not taking any medication.

Weight Watchers

As I began to talk to God about this, I heard the words "unresolved trauma" in my heart. I wondered what unresolved trauma was. A few days after hearing these words, I received an email from a health resource that shared about childhood trauma and its impact on our physical health. I could not believe what I was reading. The health resource was my confirmation. I had carried some heavyweights in my heart, my life. When I could no longer hold those heavy weights, my brain, the part of us that guides our minds, had to let go. Sometimes, the loss of a relationship through death can become a weight in our lives. The pressure circumstances bring can also become weights we carry, such as my caring for my terminally ill mom. At the beginning of 2020, I experienced the loss of an uncle, and I had a diagnosis of abnormal cells detected in my body with a previous history of cervical cancer. Reflecting on the beginning of 2019, I was in a season full of heavyweights, and I am thankful I overcame the pressures it brought me. I was so involved with both of my parents because of their life-threatening illnesses that I didn't remember the diagnosis I received. It was difficult knowing my mom and dad were near death at the same time. I am thankful my dad came out of the coma in February 2019.

My mom's death was deeply troubling and painful when she passed away in March of 2019. Despite the death of my mom, the presence of God was with me and kept me. I transitioned from sorrow to joy and peace as I encountered His presence.

During these seasons of death, I also had to create some natural encounters. In 2021, I began a walking regimen at a local 4-mile park. I am still walking today in 2024, weather permitting. With walking, I incorporated talking to God and increased my walking distance from 1 mile to 3 miles. Each day, I was receiving therapy because everything in that park spoke to me. The water, the trees, the birds, the squirrels, the sun, the flowers, the wind, the sky were so beautiful to behold.

Seeing the beauty in creation was healing for me. I also received the kindness of friendly strangers I met during those walks. It is a fantastic place that I have the privilege of accessing when I feel weighted. I think my most weighty experience was the death of my mom because I was with her during challenging moments. It was difficult for me to watch her suffer. I felt helpless, and when she cried, sometimes I cried with her. My mom and I lived states away, and I carried the weight of not living close enough to see her more frequently. As I planned my March trip to see her, I knew this would be the last time I would see her alive. On Sunday, March 3rd, I went to church at 800 am and went online to check in for my upcoming flight when I returned home. During the online check-in, I discovered my flight was not available. I have traveled for many years but have never experienced a flight cancellation. I called the airlines, and they provided me a flight that day. I was already packed and prepared for travel. I accepted the flight.

Weight Watchers

I did all the usual check-in processes at the security checkpoint and waited at the gate where I would board the plane. Nothing unusual or out of the ordinary happened. However, after we boarded the plane at the Philadelphia airport, we were delayed on the ground for an hour and a half. We missed our connecting flight when we arrived at the next airport in St. Louis. As a result of our delay from Philadelphia, every passenger aboard that flight was overnight in St. Louis. As we got off the plane in St. Louis, a stranger asked me twice if I wanted to go to a hotel with her, which seemed unusual. She was older and appeared harmless, but I said, "No, thank you." I was thinking about how I could not risk missing another flight because I didn't want to miss the opportunity to see my mom. I stayed inside the airport in St. Louis overnight and never slept. Yes, I was awake for this 24-hour trip into Texas.

As this trip unfolded, it proved to be highly unusual. The airline servicing me provided an accommodating flight that would put me into the Houston Hobby Airport and get me into my destination airport, Austin Bergstrom International. Amazingly, I met an 87 1/2 year old gentleman, Dr. Virgil Woods. He was involved in the Civil Rights Movement alongside Dr. Martin Luther King. During this first encounter, Dr. Woods knew specific things about my personality. He could only know these things if we were closely acquainted, yet we had never met till that moment.

Rejoice

That profound encounter with Dr. Woods confirmed that my travel delay and being stranded overnight was not a coincidence but divine providence.

My flight challenges happened so that I could meet Dr. Woods. We boarded the plane in Houston and sat together, and I gained insights from a great man. Dr. Woods knew his role was to impart powerful words into my hearing. What I took from my encounter with Dr. Woods is this. The timing of my being in the presence of greatness revealed that greatness was on my mom and was also upon me.

I felt incredibly blessed to have this encounter with a man who had served alongside Dr. King. I finally arrived to see my mom for 4 1/2 hours at her Nursing home, still without sleep from my lengthy travel. When I encountered my mom, it was a moment I will never forget as long as I live. Here was my opportunity to see the fragileness of life. I watched my mom slip away into the next life, and it was tough for me to let go. Do you realize that you and I do not take our breath from moment to moment in our ability? I was able to see that as I watched my mom breathe heavily, unable to speak. I remember wondering what she was thinking in those moments. I recall the shrill cries I belted out talking to her about our relationship. Telling her that it was okay to leave was difficult. I would have been satisfied to see her live a lot longer, even in the poor condition she was in. Finally, I said, "Mom, if the Lord is willing, I will see you tomorrow."

Weight Watchers

The next day, I arrived at the nursing home from my hotel nearby to see my mom still waiting for me.

I made peace with her, asking her forgiveness, and we shared 2 1/2 more hours before she exited. I watched her heavy breathing reduce and quickly become regular. Then her eyes opened extremely wide. It was as if someone had placed something in them to hold her eyes open. We were in a supernatural moment. She was having an encounter that was not visible, seeing what she had not seen before. My Mom and I were in the presence of angels. She saw angels, and the angels had come to escort her home. Her eyes followed the angels as they moved around her room, up towards the ceiling, down to my right, and then behind me. Then, in seconds, she was no longer inside her physical body. I witnessed her exit, and the life that had been inside her deteriorating body was gone. I yelled for a nurse to come quickly. I could not believe she was gone in just a moment. After watching my mom transition, I knew I would never be the same. I have seen what some people talk about.

From that moment, moving forward, my mortality has been in my face. We have the gift of time, and we must realize how fragile we are as human beings. We must not take the moments we have for granted. When I returned to Delaware, I got a free Mary Kay facial a friend offered me. After that, I did a photo shoot my church hosted for the church members directory.

Rejoice

The pictures were lovely, and as I looked at my face, I thought, wow, no one would believe I just put my mom to rest.

I did not look sorrowful, and I did not permit myself to wallow in the experience of burying my mom. I got up and went on with my life.

The experience I had with my mom's death and life before me is part of my motivation to write this book. I have learned through loss and death that I can still have joy. Joy is my choice no matter what happens.

While I may have a moment of weakness, sorrow, depression, and sadness, I will walk in the resilience my mom walked out through her life. As I remember her and my sister Sharon, I consider the things they did not get to accomplish and experience. With this always in the forefront of my thoughts, I am determined to do great things and live strong in joy and peace, not in worry and fear.

We do not have to live in despair, depression, and hopelessness. It is not over for us as long as we have the breath of life. Your life is a gift to you! Time is a precious gift, and you and I are to maximize it to accomplish our dreams and realize our destiny.

Today, mental health professionals have become overwhelmed with the challenges many people are having emotionally and psychologically as a result of the pandemic, not to mention the issues that had already happened before the pandemic. The only good I have seen from the pandemic is that it has forced people to look at their lives and choose to be involved with what is most important. People have chosen to live with a lesser income to have more time with their families. The pandemic has inspired many people to step out and launch a dream or vision into reality. What happened? Bad things can motivate us. The Bible scripture that supports this is Romans 8:28, which says all things work together for good to those who love God and to those who are called according to His purpose. I don't know your thoughts about life and the challenges you lived through. My intent is not to influence your belief system. However, I am asking you to look at your own life.

Think about how you survived the catastrophic event we have just come from without dying. A worldwide pandemic that wiped out an immeasurable number of people. What about other things you have survived that had the power to take you out of here? Put it all together and consider there is a supreme being who has faithfully kept you and others you know. What I am saying to you is vital to your living abundantly in the joy I experience. You can have it, too, but your heart must be willing to encounter the God I have been sharing about.

He will come and live in your heart if you let Him. From this, your next step is to participate in reading the Bible, His written words to know Him and discover who you are. Your life will never be the same.

I encountered Him because His love drew me through someone I did not know. He knows who you are and how to draw you in. He is everywhere, and His presence dwells in every place and thing. When I am in nature, admiring how it responds, I experience the closeness of His presence. I am in awe of the beauty He has created and highly motivated to be outdoors near the water. It is the time that I take to get in the moment. I often look back at pictures of the beautiful scenery I captured. The water is spectacular and unique when the waves are crashing. Our humanity is only sometimes as stunning as the river I visit.

We allow ourselves to become containers of evil thoughts that can manifest into wrong actions. We can choose what we want to think about. We can choose to think about bad things, circumstances, or people who make us miserable. Or we can choose to think about what brings us joy and the things we love. As I engage you in this divinely inspired conversation, may you feel better and be healthy in your whole being. It is not over yet. We are still here. The question you should ask yourself is, why am I here? I can confidently answer that question for myself, but I cannot answer that question for you.

Remember, life is your gift to live, enjoy, and experience fulfillment.

Your fulfillment is in your purpose and the things God designed you to accomplish. I want to challenge you to open your eyes and see that you have an abundant life waiting for you. I want to challenge you to open your ears to hear what you have never heard. I want you to realize you are the only one who can stop you from achieving your dream and reaching your destiny. You are the only one who can prevent you from living well. You are the only one that can destroy your forward momentum. So, my friends, laugh your way out of the negativity, the pain, the trauma, the difficulties, and the suffering others may have caused you. Lay aside wrong attitudes and wrong decisions and actions.

Be willing to give others your love but not your joy and peace. Care for your inner self, and keep the weight off your life. Then, as you continue to move towards healthy thinking to run your race in the appointed time, you will gain the capacity to REJOICE.

> *Romans 8:28* (AMP) *And we know [with great confidence] that God [who is deeply concerned about us] causes all things to work together [as a plan] for good for those who love God, to those who are called according to His plan and purpose.*

Rejoice

Ephesians 1:22-23 (NLT) God has put all things under the authority of Christ and has made him head over all things for the benefit of the church. And the church is his body; it is made full and complete by Christ, who fills all things everywhere with himself.

Hebrews 12:1 (AMP) Therefore, since we are surrounded by so great a cloud of witnesses [who by faith have testified to the truth of God's absolute faithfulness], stripping off every unnecessary weight and the sin which so easily and cleverly entangles us, let us run with endurance and active persistence the race that is set before us.

Hebrews 12:1 (AMPC) let us strip off and throw aside every encumbrance (unnecessary weight) and that sin which so readily (deftly and cleverly) clings to and entangles us, and let us run with patient endurance and steady and active persistence the appointed course of the race that is set before us.

Chapter 9

Spark Joy

Because of you; I know the path of life as I taste the fullness of joy in your presence. At your right side, I experience divine pleasures forevermore! Get into the presence of God, and you will spark joy. In His presence is the fullness of joy. Imagine having so much of this joy inside that you are full. The presence of Yahweh is waiting to hear your worship. It is the posture of praise that manifests joy. You engage His presence, the presence of God, with singing! When you choose the posture of praise, the Holy Spirit, the Spirit of Truth, will come. He is the one who brings joy to you. He is here to comfort you in your mourning season. He is here to give you beauty for your ashes and the oil of joy. He comes to help you make an exchange. You give Him your sorrow, and He gives you joy through your worship. When you praise Him, the heaviness you feel will go. On March 2, 2023, while singing, I sensed the presence of the Holy Spirit. I began to laugh and laugh. The laughter was a continuous, deep laughter. What happened? The Holy Spirit showed up, zapping me with joy while I worshiped!

Rejoice

It was a beautiful encounter. I had not laughed like that in many years. That evening, I shared this scripture in a spiritual gathering to encourage the people I stood before. Proverbs 4:20-23 (TPT) Listen carefully, my dear child, to everything that I teach you, and pay attention to all that I have to say. Fill your thoughts with my words until they penetrate deep into your spirit. Then, as you unwrap my words, they will impart true life and radiant health into the very core of your being. So, above all, guard the affections of your heart, for they affect all that you are. Pay attention to the welfare of your innermost being; from there, the wellspring of life flows.

I have meditated on this scripture since 2012 and received revelation several times. March 2, 2023, was one of those times. The key takeaway is that our inner self requires our attention and protection. We often get into trouble through our words because we have not protected our innermost being, our heart. This part of us includes our thoughts, emotions, and motives.

Another revelation from this scripture is that we will receive good health in our inner self, which is the core of our being.

Can you see from this scripture how our thoughts and words affect physical and emotional health? Look at this same scripture in the ERV translation, the Easy-to-Read Version.

Proverbs 4:20-23 (ERV) *My son, pay attention to what I say. Listen closely to my words. Don't let them out of your sight. Never stop thinking about them. These words are the secret of life and health to all who discover them. Above all, be careful what you think because your thoughts control your life.*

In this translation, we see the two insights I shared more clearly. The first insight is to keep the Bible's words with you and meditate on them. When you think about the scripture and speak it aloud, you meditate on it. What happens when you meditate on anything? Whatever you roll over in your heart or inner self will hurt or build you. Another way to put this is that we will have life according to what we ponder in our thoughts. That is a sobering statement. If I meditate on negativity, my life will attract negative people and circumstances.

If what we let enter our inner selves is harmful, toxic, and unhealthy, we will become physically and emotionally sick. Think of this like physical food. We must eat physical food to sustain our bodies, or we will eventually die physically. We must partake of Bible scripture to sustain us physically and emotionally. Wow, the words of the Bible have the power to keep us physically and emotionally healthy when we engage them. This scripture I am sharing from Proverbs 4:20-23 is in my heart, inner self, thoughts, and emotions.

Rejoice

When I shared this insight on March 2, 2023, as a message of encouragement to the people, I also brought the presence of joy. Joy was all over me, and everyone in that meeting experienced its tangible presence. How did that happen? My worship unto God, Yahweh, earlier that day brought the presence of the Holy Spirit, and He ignited the presence of His joy within me. The Holy Spirit is our partner in all things spiritual, and He is present to help you navigate your everyday life. He always operates in conjunction with the Bible scriptures. His presence and the scriptures I had meditated on caused Yahweh's joy to remain with me. Another revelation in this scripture text of the ERV translation is that whatever we think about controls our lives, so we must keep our thoughts sound.

Looking at this insight, we can reflect on what the Apostle Paul said in Philippians 4:8. Fix your thoughts and think about things that are lovely, just, true, honest, pure, and of a good report. Our soul, which is the seat of our mind, will, emotions, and intellect, can be well if we protect it. Your soul is the part of you that evil seeks to access because if you can be compromised, you will live defeated. What are you paying attention to? What is it that you let enter your sight? What are you listening to? Your eyes and ears are gates to your heart, your inner self. Become a watchdog over your inner self.

When something enters your heart, it comes through your eyes or ears. Screen and check everything you see and hear to prevent the robbery of your peace. Peace is your weapon of protection.

Peace protects your inner self and mind from releasing negativity you saw or heard. If you permit negativity to enter through your ear and eye gates once you digest it, you will release it. It is just like eating food.

Once we have eaten the food, it must eventually be released. Otherwise, we would get sick if we could not release it. It is the same with the negative imagery and information you digest.

If you get too full of it, you cannot contain it. As a result, releasing what you receive will shape your life to move in a negative direction. There is an evil strategy at work here.

If you receive what enters your ear and eye gates, you speak it out, and your spoken words shape your life's course. God did not design us to receive negativity in our ears and eye gates. Negativity is unhealthy for our hearts or inner self, just like foods with nasty ingredients are harmful to our bodies. The word of God is our strategy against negative imagery and communication. Your soul is valuable to God. God wants you to know how much He cares about you.

Rejoice

He cares about everything in your life, and everything about your life matters to Him. God knows what you need and wants you to prosper in every area of your being: your mind, will, emotions, spirit, and body. God is faithful. He will not forget you and will not abandon you. Are you willing to engage in dialogue with me? If so, then repeat these words after me so they will get into your heart. God cares about me. God cares about everything in my life. God cares about what matters to me. God cares about what I need. God knows what I need. God cares about what matters to me, from small, insignificant, and significant things. He will not forget me. God will not abandon me. God wants me to prosper in my mind, will, emotions, spirit, and body! Allow your words to resonate in your heart and change your negative thinking. Through the written words of the Bible, God wants to speak to the life we are living inside, the life in our innermost being, the real you and me. His words can change our thoughts and transform our minds. It can pull out the harmful garbage we digested and bring us to wholeness. Listening closely to Bible scriptures, as you say it out loud, is how to get it into your inner self. It is like hearing a song for the first time, and you listen closely to the words, and in 2 seconds flat, you are singing the song. You are likely not listening if you say you tried this and it didn't work. Get into a quiet place, give it your full attention, and speak it aloud repeatedly. Do this regularly, just like eating or taking your medication. Remember, this weapon activates joy and peace in your inner self. You will be changed when you deploy this weapon.

The word of God, when deployed, releases two crucial weapons in your arsenal: joy and peace.

Joy strengthens your mind and thoughts, while Peace protects your mind and thoughts. Remember, what we speak comes from our thoughts; our wrong thoughts control our lives. I want to share one more translation of Proverbs 4:23 with you. The Passion translation shares the verse this way: Listen carefully, my dear child, to everything that I teach you, and pay attention to all that I have to say. Fill your thoughts with my words until they penetrate deep into your spirit. Then, as you unwrap my words, they will impart true life and radiant health into the very core of your being. So, above all, guard the affections of your heart, for they affect all that you are.

Pay attention to the welfare of your innermost being, for the wellspring of life flows from there. Notice that the words pay attention are mentioned twice in this scripture. There are two instructions for us to follow. The first instruction is to pay attention to what the word of God, the Bible, is saying.

The second instruction is to pay attention to our innermost being, our inner self. Another instruction in this verse is we must fill our thoughts with God's word until His word penetrates deep into our spirit. Why should we follow this instruction? Because the word of God will impart true life and radiant health into the very core of our being.

Rejoice

The latter part of verse 23 says the wellspring of life flows from there. Out of our hearts flows the seasons of life. The Hebrew word yasa is the word season, specifically springtime. What shapes the seasons of our lives? People think their age or circumstances shape the seasons of our lives.

It is our hearts or our inner selves that shape the seasons of our lives. If we keep our hearts right before God, we can live in perpetual springtime, meaning we can live in a never-ending, continuous, persistent springtime, resulting in an ongoing life of beauty. You do not have to live another day without God's peace and joy occupying your heart and inner self. The struggle we all face is in our minds, but He has provided everything we need to win. However, this does require our participation in His word, the Bible. His word is a significant key to living an overcoming life of victory filled with joy and peace. Can I ask you to engage in dialogue with me again? If you are willing, would you say this simple prayer? What we are doing is engaging Yahweh, God, with our hearts and our words. Father, Here's my heart. Forgive me for having evil thoughts about others. I forgive those who have wronged me, and I let it go. Cleanse my heart from all evil and change me from the inside out! Help me to make your word a priority above all other books.

I surrender all I am to your Holy Spirit in Jesus's name. Amen. I want to thank you for praying with me. I encourage you to invest in yourself.

Purchase a quality bible with a translation you can understand. If you cannot purchase a Bible, there are local churches you can ask to provide one. One of the most important things you can do to experience a fulfilled life is to read and study the Bible. If you want to encounter God, the Bible will reveal who He is, How He thinks about things, and who you are. Developing a personal relationship with Him is vital because you will discover in your friendship that He will not lie to you, cheat you, put you down, or remind you of your mistakes. You will experience Him and become a force to contend with. Become a lover of the one who loves you. Give your love to Him even though you have never seen Him. Though you do not see Him now, you can trust Him, and as you trust Him, you will Rejoice with a glorious, inexpressible joy! May your heart be willing and obedient to everything I have shared so you may eat the good of the land.

So pray like this, 'God, our father, you live in heaven. We want everyone to respect you. We want you to be everyone's boss. We want everyone in the world to do what you want, just like everyone in heaven does what you want. Please give us the food that we need each day. Please don't punish us for the bad things that we did, just like we don't do payback to the people that did bad things to us. Don't let anything push us to do bad things. And keep us safe from the devil, the boss over the bad spirits.' "Amen.

Rejoice

Psalms 16:11 (TPT) Because of you, I know the path of life, as I taste the fullness of joy in your presence. At your right side I experience divine pleasures forevermore!

Isaiah 61:3 (KJV) to appoint unto them that mourn in Zion, to give unto them beauty for ashes, the oil of joy for mourning, the garment of praise for the spirit of heaviness; that they might be called trees of righteousness, the planting of the Lord, that he might be glorified.

John 16:13 (NLT) When the Spirit of truth comes, he will guide you into all truth. He will not speak on his own but will tell you what he has heard. He will tell you about the future.

Proverbs 4:20-23 (TPT) Listen carefully, my dear child, to everything that I teach you, and pay attention to all that I have to say. Fill your thoughts with my words until they penetrate deep into your spirit. Then, as you unwrap my words, they will impart true life and radiant health into the very core of your being. So above all, guard the affections of your heart, for they affect all that you are. Pay attention to the welfare of your innermost being, for the wellspring of life flows from there.

Luke 12:6-7 (TPT) "What is the value of your soul to God? Could any amount of money define your worth? God doesn't abandon or forget even the small sparrow he has made. How then could he forget or abandon you? What about the seemingly minor issues of your life? Do they matter to God? Of course they do! So you never need to worry, for you are more valuable to God than anything else.

Philippians 4:7 (AMP) And the peace of God [that peace which reassures the heart, that peace] which transcends all understanding, [that peace which] stands guard over your hearts and your minds in Christ Jesus [is yours].

Romans 15:13 (NIV) May the God of hope fill you with all joy and peace as you trust in him, so that you may overflow with hope by the power of the Holy Spirit.

Isaiah 1:19 (NKJV) If you are willing and obedient, You shall eat the good of the land;

1 Peter 1:8 (NLT) You love him even though you have never seen him. Though you do not see him now, you trust him, and you rejoice with a glorious, inexpressible joy.

Rejoice

Matthew 6:9-13 (PEV) So pray like this. 'God, our father, you live in heaven. We want everyone to respect you. We want you to be everyone's boss. We want everyone in the world to do what you want, just like everyone in heaven does what you want. Please give us the food that we need each day. Please don't punish us for the bad things that we did, just like we don't do payback to the people that did bad things to us. Don't let anything push us to do bad things. And keep us safe from the devil, the boss over the bad spirits.' "Amen.

www.ingramcontent.com/pod-product-compliance
Lightning Source LLC
Chambersburg PA
CBHW041310240426
43661CB00064B/2888